Cloud Computing and Storage Management

Prof. Prashant Shriram Gumgaonkar

SPI PUBLICATIONS

Published by **SPI Publications**, www.spipublications.in

SPI, the **SPI logo**, and **Split Poetry India** are trademarks of **SPI Publications**, or its affiliates.

ISBN-13: 978-93-49860-40-7

First Edition 2025

SPI Publications

Corporate & Editorial Office
117/2, Sector 37, Khandsa Road,
Gurgaon, Haryana 122 001
Phone: +91 98355 52940
Email: contact@spipublications.in
Website: www.spipublications.in

Processed and Printed in India

Course Title: Cloud Computing and Storage Management

Course Objectives:

1. To learn the concept of cloud computing.
2. To understand the trade-off between deploying applications in the cloud over local infrastructure.
3. To identify different storage virtualization technologies and their benefits.
4. To understand and articulate business continuity solutions including backup and recovery technologies, local and remote replication solutions.

Course Outcomes:

After learning the course, the student will be able:

1. To understand the key dimensions of the challenge of Cloud Computing.
2. To assess the economics, financial and technological implications for selecting cloud computing for organization.
3. To describe and apply storage technologies.
4. To identify leading storage technologies that provide cost-effective IT solutions for medium to large scale businesses and data centers.
5. To describe important storage technology features such as availability, replication, scalability and performance.

Course Content:

UNIT I

Introduction: Distributed Computing and Enabling Technologies, Cloud Fundamentals: Cloud Definition, Evolution, Architecture, Applications, Deployment models and service models.

UNIT II

Virtualization: Issues with virtualization, Virtualization technologies and architectures, Internals of virtual machine monitors/hypervisors, Virtualization of data centers and Issues with Multi-tenancy, Storage virtualization, Challenges, Types of storage virtualization.

UNIT III

Implementation: Study of Cloud computing Systems like Amazon EC2 and S3, Google App Engine and Microsoft Azure, Build Private/Hybrid Cloud using open source tools, Deployment of Web Services from inside and outside a Cloud Architecture, MapReduce and its extensions to Cloud Computing, Hadoop, HDFS and GFS.

UNIT IV

Business Continuity and Recovery: Information Availability, Life cycle, Failure analysis: Backup and Recovery- Backup purpose, considerations, Backup Granularity, Recovery considerations- Backup methods, Process, backup and restore operations, Overview of emerging technologies: Duplication, Off site backup.

UNIT V

Storage security and Management: Storage security framework, Securing the Storage infrastructure, Risk triad: Managing the storage infrastructure, Monitoring the storage infrastructure, identify key parameters and components to monitor in a storage infrastructure, List key management activities and examples, Define storage management standards and initiative-Industry trend.

……………………………………………………………………………………………..

UNIT I: DISTRIBUTED COMPUTING AND CLOUD FUNDAMENTALS

What is Cloud Computing

Cloud computing is the provision of computing services such as servers, storage, databases, networking, software, analytics, and intelligence over the Internet to facilitate faster innovation, flexible resources, or economies of scale. On-demand delivery of IT resources over the Internet is referred to as cloud computing..

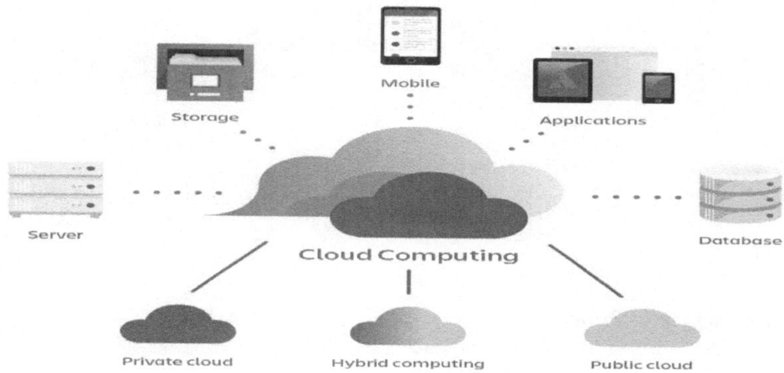

Fig: Cloud Computing

The term cloud computing encompasses hosted services that include data storage, servers, databases, networking (or software) and software running on the internet. Data is stored on physical servers, which are maintained by a cloud service provider.

Who is using cloud computing

A broad spectrum of uses, spanning from data backup to disaster recovery, email and virtual desktops (and including cloud computing), software development and testing across industries and big data analytics on customer-facing web applications are all part of the use case for the cloud. The cloud is being employed by healthcare organizations to design customized therapies for patients. Real-time fraud detection and prevention are being enabled by the cloud for financial services companies. Using the cloud, video game manufacturers are distributing their online games to millions of users globally.

Benefits of Cloud Computing

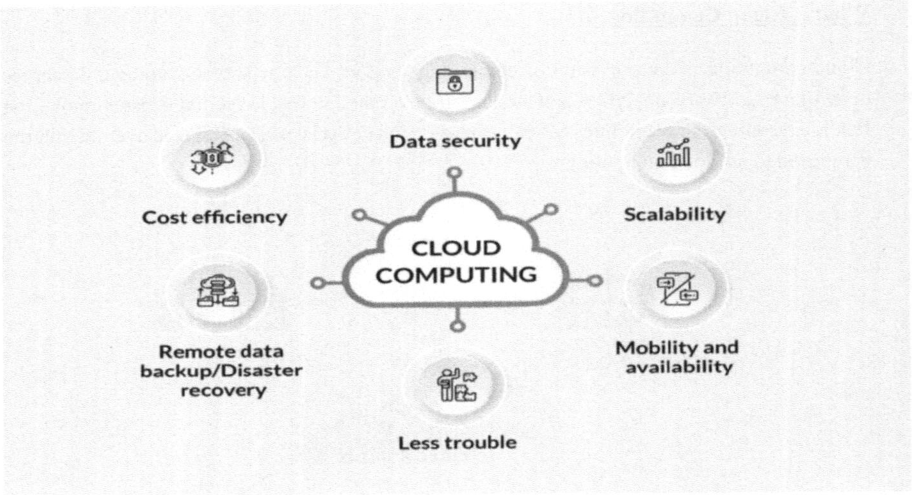

- **Faster Launch of Projects**
  - You can start or stop cloud services within seconds.
  - Developers can quickly build and test new ideas without waiting for hardware or buying new equipment.
- **Easy to Scale**
  - You can increase or decrease storage and computing power as needed.
  - No need to buy big servers—you only use what you need when you need it.
- **Saves Money**
  - You only pay for what you use.
  - No extra cost for unused servers or systems.
  - IT staff can focus on important tasks instead of managing hardware.
- **Better Teamwork**
  - Files and data stored in the cloud can be accessed from anywhere.
  - Teams can work together even from different locations or devices.
- **Stronger Security**
  - Top cloud providers use strong security systems and hire expert professionals.
  - They offer automatic updates and better protection from cyber threats.

- **Data Backup and Protection**
    - Cloud services offer backup and recovery options.
    - In case of accidents, viruses, or hardware failure, your data stays safe.
- **Flexibility**
    - Customize services based on your needs.
    - Access apps and data from any location with internet.
- **Speed and Efficiency**
    - You can bring apps or services to market quickly.
    - No need to worry about servers or infrastructure.
- **Modern Technology Advantage**
    - Cloud keeps you updated with the latest technologies.
    - Helps you stay ahead in competition.
- **Easy Access**
    - Use your data anytime, anywhere with an internet connection.
    - Supports remote work and smooth operations.
- **Mobile-Friendly**
    - Access your cloud data easily on smartphones and tablets.
    - Increases productivity even on the move.

Types of Cloud Computing

Cloud computing can either be classified based on the deployment model or the type of service. Based on the specific deployment model, we can classify cloud as public, private, and hybrid cloud. At the same time, it can be classified as infrastructure-as-a-service (IaaS), platform-as-a-service (PaaS), and software-as-a-service (SaaS) based on the service the cloud model offers.

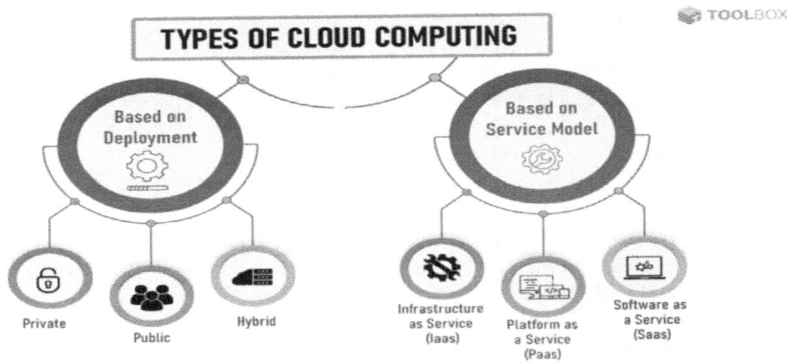

Cloud Deployment Model

Essentially, it operates as a virtual computing environment and offers varying deployment models that consider the quantity of data and access to the Infrastructure. Different Cloud Computing deployment models are available. To facilitate rapid loading, cloud hubs typically have tens of thousands of servers and storage devices. Often, users can choose to have access to data in a more specific geographic area. The classification of cloud computing deployment models is determined by their geographical location. We'll begin by examining the different types to determine which one would be appropriate for the requirements of your organization.

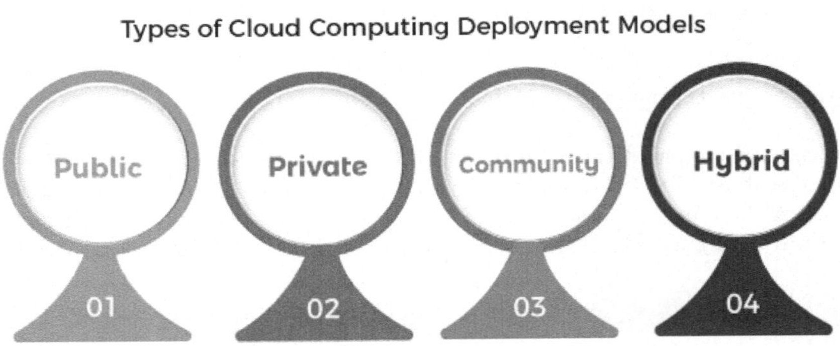

Public Cloud

The name says it all. It is accessible to the public. Public deployment models in the cloud are perfect for organizations with growing and fluctuating demands. It also makes a great choice for companies with low-security concerns. Thus, you pay a cloud service provider for networking services, compute virtualization & storage available on the public internet. It is also a great delivery model for the teams with development and testing. Its configuration and deployment are quick and easy, making it an ideal choice for test environments.Examples of public cloud are **amazon web service**, **Microsoft Azure, google cloud platform etc.**

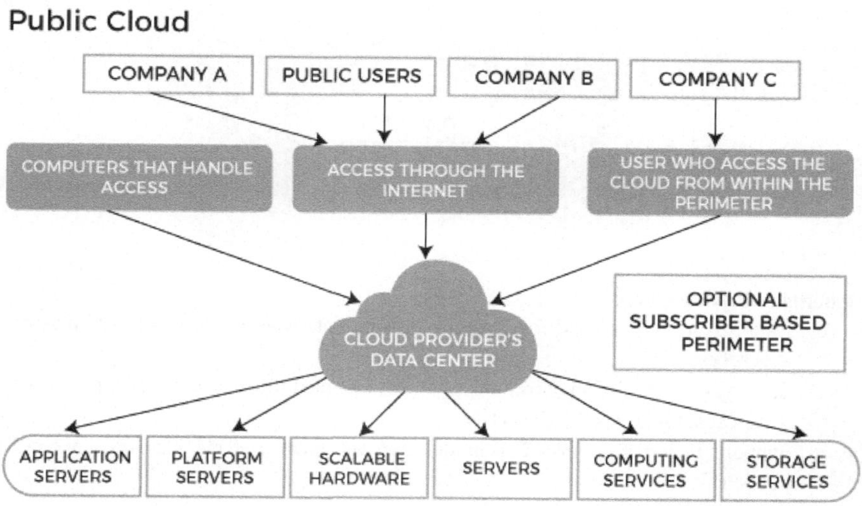

Benefits of Public Cloud

- Minimal Investment - As a pay-per-use service, there is no large upfront cost and is ideal for businesses who need quick access to resources
- No Hardware Setup - The cloud service providers fully fund the entire Infrastructure
- No Infrastructure Management - This does not require an in-house team to utilize the public cloud.

Limitations of Public Cloud

- Data Security and Privacy Concerns - Since it is accessible to all, it does not fully protect against cyber-attacks and could lead to vulnerabilities.
- Reliability Issues - Since the same server network is open to a wide range of users, it can lead to malfunction and outages
- Service/License Limitation - While there are many resources you can exchange with tenants, there is a usage cap.

Private Cloud

Now that you understand what the public cloud could offer you, of course, you are keen to know what a private cloud can do. Companies that look for cost efficiency and greater control over data & resources will find the private cloud a more suitable choice.

It means that it will be integrated with your data center and managed by your IT team. Alternatively, you can also choose to host it externally. The private cloud offers bigger opportunities that help meet specific organizations' requirements when it comes to customization. It's also a wise choice for mission-critical processes that may have frequently changing requirements.IBM , Oracle are the examples of private cloud.

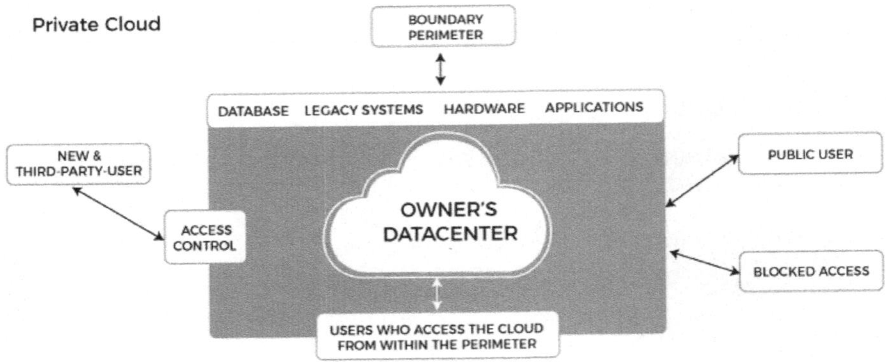

Benefits of Private Cloud

- Data Privacy - It is ideal for storing corporate data where only authorized personnel gets access
- Security - Segmentation of resources within the same Infrastructure can help with better access and higher levels of security.
- Supports Legacy Systems - This model supports legacy systems that cannot access the public cloud.

Limitations of Private Cloud

- Higher Cost - With the benefits you get, the investment will also be larger than the public cloud. Here, you will pay for software, hardware, and resources for staff and training.
- Fixed Scalability - The hardware you choose will accordingly help you scale in a certain direction
- High Maintenance - Since it is managed in-house, the maintenance costs also increase.

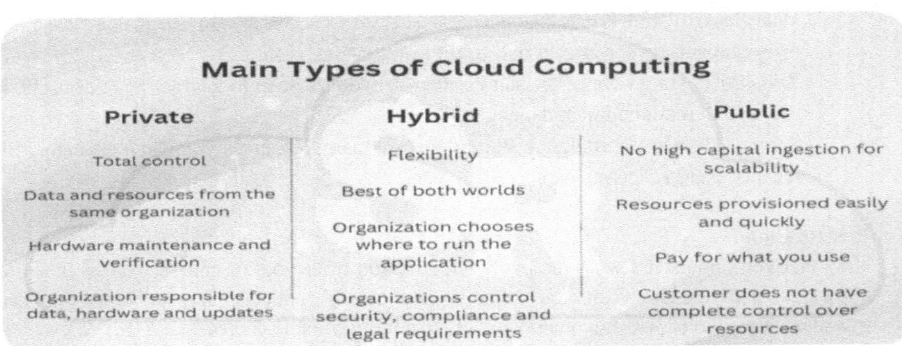

Community Cloud

The community cloud operates in a way that is similar to the public cloud. There's just one difference - it allows access to only a specific set of users who share common objectives and use cases. This type of deployment model of cloud computing is managed and hosted internally or by a third-party vendor. However, you can also choose a combination of all three.

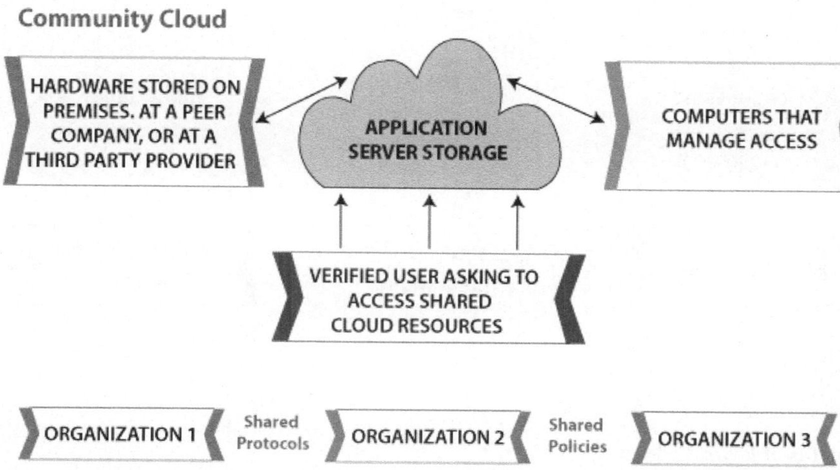

Benefits of Community Cloud

- Smaller Investment - A community cloud is much cheaper than the private & public cloud and provides great performance
- Setup Benefits - The protocols and configuration of a community cloud must align with industry standards, allowing customers to work much more efficiently.

Limitations of Community Cloud

- Shared Resources - Due to restricted bandwidth and storage capacity, community resources often pose challenges.
- Not as Popular - Since this is a recently introduced model, it is not that popular or available across industries

Hybrid Cloud

As the name suggests, a hybrid cloud is a combination of two or more cloud architectures. While each model in the hybrid cloud functions differently, it is all part of the same architecture. Further, as part of this deployment of the cloud computing model, the internal or external providers can offer resources.

Let's understand the hybrid model better. A company with critical data will prefer storing on a private cloud, while less sensitive data can be stored on a public cloud. The hybrid cloud is also frequently used for 'cloud bursting'. It means, supposes an organization runs an application on-premises, but due to heavy load, it can burst into the public cloud.

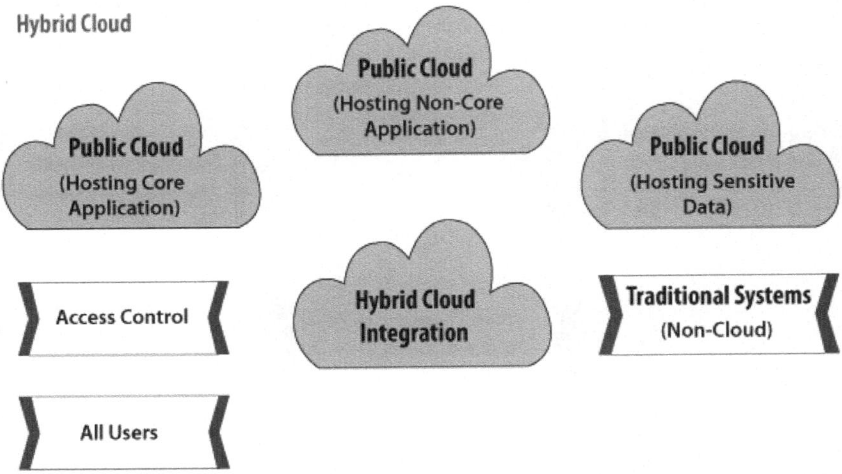

Benefits of Hybrid Cloud

- Cost-Effectiveness - The overall cost of a hybrid solution decreases since it majorly uses the public cloud to store data.
- Security - Since data is properly segmented, the chances of data theft from attackers are significantly reduced.
- Flexibility - With higher levels of flexibility, businesses can create custom solutions that fit their exact requirements

Limitations of Hybrid Cloud

- Complexity - It is complex setting up a hybrid cloud since it needs to integrate two or more cloud architectures
- Specific Use Case - This model makes more sense for organizations that have multiple use cases or need to separate critical and sensitive data

A Comparative Analysis of Cloud Deployment Models

With the below table, we have attempted to analyze the key models with an overview of what each one can do for you:

Important Factors to Consider	Public	Private	Community	Hybrid
Setup and ease of use	Easy	Requires professional IT Team	Requires professional IT Team	Requires professional IT Team
Data Security and Privacy	Low	High	Very High	High

Scalability and flexibility	High	High	Fixed requirements	High
Cost-Effectiveness	Most affordable	Most expensive	Cost is distributed among members	Cheaper than private but more expensive than public
Reliability	Low	High	Higher	High

Based on Service Model Cloud divided into three types :-

Software as a Service (SaaS) – It is also known as **cloud application services**. Mostly, SaaS applications run directly through the web browser means we do not require to download and install these applications. Some important example of SaaS is given below –
Example: Google Apps, Salesforce Dropbox, Slack, Hubspot, Cisco WebEx.

Platform as a Service (PaaS) – It is also known as **cloud platform services**. It is quite similar to SaaS, but the difference is that PaaS provides a platform for software creation, but using SaaS, we can access software over the internet without the need of any platform.
Example: Windows Azure, Force.com, Magento Commerce Cloud, OpenShift.

Infrastructure as a Service (IaaS) – It is also known as **cloud infrastructure services**. It is responsible for managing applications data, middleware, and runtime environments.
Example: Amazon Web Services (AWS) EC2, Google Compute Engine (GCE), Cisco Metapod.

Cloud Computing Architecture

Cloud computing architecture is a combination of **service-oriented architecture** and **event-driven architecture**.

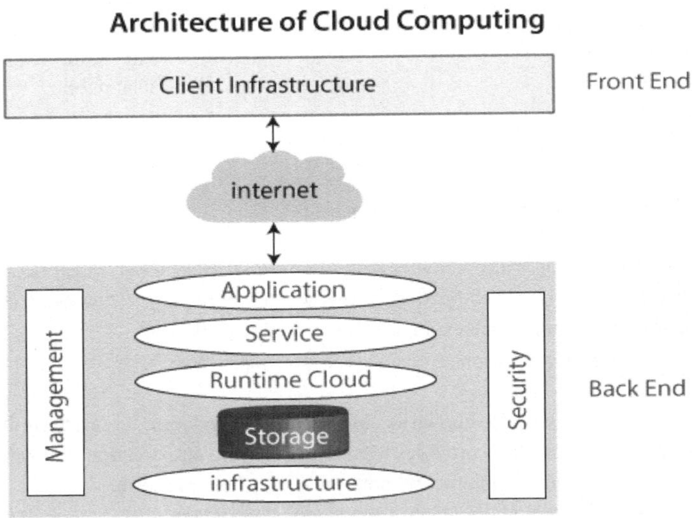

Front End

The front end is used by the client. It contains client-side interfaces and applications that are required to access the cloud computing platforms. The front end includes web servers (including Chrome, Firefox, internet explorer, etc.), thin & fat clients, tablets, and mobile devices.

Back End

The back end is used by the service provider. It manages all the resources that are required to provide cloud computing services. It includes a huge amount of data storage, security mechanism, virtual machines, deploying models, servers, traffic control mechanisms, etc.

Components of Cloud Computing Architecture

There are the following components of cloud computing architecture -

1. Client Infrastructure

Client Infrastructure is a Front end component. It provides GUI (Graphical User Interface) to interact with the cloud.

2. Application

The application may be any software or platform that a client wants to access.

3. Service

A Cloud Services manages that which type of service you access according to the client's requirement.

Cloud computing offers the following three type of services:

i. Software as a Service (SaaS) – It is also known as **cloud application services**. Mostly, SaaS applications run directly through the web browser means we do not require to download and install these applications. Some important example of SaaS is given below –

Example: Google Apps, Salesforce Dropbox, Slack, Hubspot, Cisco WebEx.

ii. Platform as a Service (PaaS) – It is also known as **cloud platform services**. It is quite similar to SaaS, but the difference is that PaaS provides a platform for software creation, but using SaaS, we can access software over the internet without the need of any platform.

Example: Windows Azure, Force.com, Magento Commerce Cloud, OpenShift.

iii. Infrastructure as a Service (IaaS) – It is also known as **cloud infrastructure services**. It is responsible for managing applications data, middleware, and runtime environments.

Example: Amazon Web Services (AWS) EC2, Google Compute Engine (GCE), Cisco Metapod.

4. Runtime Cloud

Runtime Cloud provides the **execution and runtime environment** to the virtual machines.

5. Storage

Storage is one of the most important components of cloud computing. It provides a huge amount of storage capacity in the cloud to store and manage data.

6. Infrastructure

It provides services on the **host level**, **application level**, and **network level**. Cloud infrastructure includes hardware and software components such as servers, storage, network devices, virtualization software, and other storage resources that are needed to support the cloud computing model.

7. Management

Management is used to manage components such as application, service, runtime cloud, storage, infrastructure, and other security issues in the backend and establish coordination between them.

8.**Security**

Security is an in-built back end component of cloud computing. It implements a security mechanism in the back end.

9. Internet

The Internet is medium through which front end and back end can interact and communicate with each other.

Cloud Service Models

There are the following three types of cloud service models -

1. Infrastructure as a Service (IaaS)
2. Platform as a Service (PaaS)
3. Software as a Service (SaaS)

- **Infrastructure as a Service (IaaS)**

IaaS is also known as **Hardware as a Service (HaaS)**. It is a computing infrastructure managed over the internet. The main advantage of using IaaS is that it helps users to avoid the cost and complexity of purchasing and managing the physical servers.

Characteristics of IaaS

There are the following characteristics of IaaS -

- Resources are available as a service
- Services are highly scalable
- Dynamic and flexible
- GUI and API-based access
- Automated administrative tasks

Example: DigitalOcean, Linode, Amazon Web Services (AWS), Microsoft Azure, Google Compute Engine (GCE), Rackspace, and Cisco Metacloud.

- **Platform as a Service (PaaS)**

PaaS cloud computing platform is created for the programmer to develop, test, run, and manage the applications.

Characteristics of PaaS

There are the following characteristics of PaaS -

- Accessible to various users via the same development application.
- Integrates with web services and databases.
- Builds on virtualization technology, so resources can easily be scaled up or down as per the organization's need.
- Support multiple languages and frameworks.
- Provides an ability to "**Auto-scale**".

Example: AWS Elastic Beanstalk, Windows Azure, Heroku, Force.com, Google App Engine, Apache Stratos, Magento Commerce Cloud, and OpenShift.

- **Software as a Service (SaaS)**

SaaS is also known as "**on-demand software**". It is a software in which the applications are hosted by a cloud service provider. Users can access these applications with the help of internet connection and web browser.

Characteristics of SaaS

There are the following characteristics of SaaS -

- Managed from a central location
- Hosted on a remote server
- Accessible over the internet
- Users are not responsible for hardware and software updates. Updates are applied automatically.

- The services are purchased on the pay-as-per-use basis

Example: BigCommerce, Google Apps, Salesforce, Dropbox, ZenDesk, Cisco WebEx, ZenDesk, Slack, and GoToMeeting.

Difference between IaaS, PaaS, and SaaS

The below table shows the difference between IaaS, PaaS, and SaaS -

IaaS	Paas	SaaS
It provides a virtual data center to store information and create platforms for app development, testing, and deployment.	It provides virtual platforms and tools to create, test, and deploy apps.	It provides web software and apps to complete business tasks.
It provides access to resources such as virtual machines, virtual storage, etc.	It provides runtime environments and deployment tools for applications.	It provides software as a service to the end-users.
It is used by network architects.	It is used by developers.	It is used by end users.
IaaS provides only Infrastructure.	PaaS provides Infrastructure+Platform.	SaaS provides Infrastructure+Platform +Software.

Advantages of Cloud Service Models

Cost Efficiency: Cloud providers provide a pricing model that permits customers to pay only for the sources they consume.

Scalability: Cloud services provide the potential to scale sources up or down speedily and respond to changing workloads and commercial organization requirements. This flexibility ensures that agencies can correctly manipulate fluctuating needs without over-provisioning.

Accessibility and Flexibility: Cloud computing allows one to get access to applications and facts remotely from everywhere with an internet connection. This fosters collaboration among geographically dispersed groups and allows users to work flexibly.

Rapid Deployment: Cloud provider models facilitate rapid deployment of programs. Users can provision sources and deploy programs quickly, decreasing time-to-market and allowing faster innovation.

Managed Services: Cloud providers offer more than a few managed offerings, managing duties together with safety, tracking, and safety.

Automatic Updates and Patch Management: Cloud providers manipulate software application updates, patches, and protection functions robotically.

Disadvantages of Cloud Service Models

Security Concerns: Security remains a top concern for companies moving to the cloud. Storing information and programs on out-of-door servers will increase questions on statistics' privateness, regulatory compliance, and the functionality of unauthorized access.
Dependency on Internet Connectivity: Cloud services require a reliable internet connection. Downtime or disruptions in internet connectivity can impact the right to access essential applications and information, affecting business operations.
Limited Customization in SaaS: While SaaS offers convenience, it is able to lack the extent of customization that a few organizations require.
Data Transfer Costs: Moving huge volumes of records from the cloud can require extra charges.
Vendor Lock-In: Adopting certain cloud providers can also result in provider lock-in, wherein it becomes hard to migrate packages and statistics to a different employer or again to on-premises surroundings.
Potential for Downtime: Cloud company companies may also experience outages or downtime, impacting the supply of services.

SAMPLE MCQ QUESTIONS AND ANSWER

Section 1: Distributed Computing and Enabling Technologies

1. **Which of the following best defines distributed computing?**
   a) Computing that is done only on a single machine
   b) Multiple computers working independently
   c) A system where processing is done on multiple networked computers
   d) Centralized processing for large-scale computation
   Answer: c) A system where processing is done on multiple networked computers
2. **Which of the following is NOT an enabling technology of distributed computing?**
   a) Web Services
   b) Virtualization
   c) GPS Tracking
   d) Middleware
   Answer: c) GPS Tracking
3. **In distributed systems, what is the role of middleware?**
   a) It replaces the operating system
   b) It connects users to the cloud directly
   c) It manages network routing
   d) It acts as a bridge between different software components
   Answer: d) It acts as a bridge between different software components
4. **Which is an example of distributed computing?**
   a) Single user PC
   b) Google Search Engine
   c) BIOS software
   d) MS Word
   Answer: b) Google Search Engine

Section 2: Cloud Definition & Evolution

5. **What is Cloud Computing?**
   a) Computing using physical storage only
   b) A model for enabling on-demand network access to shared computing resources
   c) A desktop application model
   d) A form of embedded system
   Answer: b) A model for enabling on-demand network access to shared computing resources
6. **Cloud computing evolved primarily from which earlier technology?**
   a) Bluetooth
   b) Grid computing
   c) IoT
   d) Blockchain
   Answer: b) Grid computing
7. **Which of the following is a key characteristic of cloud computing?**
   a) Manual provisioning
   b) Fixed pricing
   c) On-demand self-service
   d) Offline storage only
   Answer: c) On-demand self-service
8. **Who coined the term "Cloud Computing"?**
   a) IBM
   b) Amazon
   c) Google
   d) No single person or company
   Answer: d) No single person or company

Section 3: Cloud Architecture

9. **Which of the following is NOT a layer of cloud computing architecture?**
   a) Infrastructure layer
   b) Application layer
   c) Hardware layer
   d) Management layer
   Answer: c) Hardware layer
10. **The cloud architecture consists of which three major components?**
    a) Clients, Data Centers, Distributed Networks
    b) Clients, Hardware, Operating Systems
    c) Browsers, Middleware, Platforms
    d) Servers, Software, Filesystems
    Answer: a) Clients, Data Centers, Distributed Networks

Section 4: Cloud Applications

11. **Which of the following is a common cloud-based application?**
    a) Microsoft Excel offline
    b) Notepad
    c) Google Docs
    d) VLC Media Player
    Answer: c) Google Docs
12. **Which industry benefits the most from cloud applications in terms of scalability?**
    a) Agriculture
    b) Healthcare
    c) Textile
    d) Mining
    Answer: b) Healthcare

Section 5: Deployment Models

13. **Which deployment model provides cloud services to the general public?**
    a) Private Cloud
    b) Public Cloud
    c) Hybrid Cloud
    d) Community Cloud
    Answer: b) Public Cloud
14. **Which cloud deployment model is shared by several organizations with common goals?**
    a) Public Cloud
    b) Hybrid Cloud
    c) Private Cloud
    d) Community Cloud
    Answer: d) Community Cloud
15. **Which deployment model combines both private and public clouds?**
    a) Community Cloud
    b) Hybrid Cloud
    c) Public Cloud
    d) Consolidated Cloud
    Answer: b) Hybrid Cloud

Section 6: Service Models

16. **Which cloud model provides software over the internet?**
    a) IaaS
    b) PaaS
    c) SaaS
    d) NaaS
    Answer: c) SaaS

17. **Which of the following is an example of IaaS?**
    a) Microsoft Word
    b) Dropbox
    c) Amazon EC2
    d) Google Docs
    Answer: c) Amazon EC2
18. **Which service model is most suitable for developers to build applications without worrying about infrastructure?**
    a) SaaS
    b) IaaS
    c) PaaS
    d) DaaS
    Answer: c) PaaS
19. **Which cloud model provides only hardware-level services like storage, servers, and networking?**
    a) SaaS
    b) IaaS
    c) PaaS
    d) HaaS
    Answer: b) IaaS
20. **Which of the following is an example of SaaS?**
    a) Microsoft Azure
    b) Google App Engine
    c) Dropbox
    d) Amazon EC2
    Answer: c) Dropbox

Unit No. 2 VIRTUALIZATION

Virtualization is technology that you can use to create virtual representations of servers, storage, networks, and other physical machines.
Virtualization is used to create a virtual version of an underlying service With the help of Virtualization, multiple operating systems and applications can run on the same machine and its same hardware at the same time, increasing the utilization and flexibility of hardware. It was initially developed during the mainframe era.
It is one of the main cost-effective, hardware-reducing, and energy-saving techniques used by cloud providers. Virtualization allows sharing of a single physical instance of a resource or an application among multiple customers and organizations at one time.

Virtualization example

Consider a company that needs servers for three functions:

1. Store business email securely
2. Run a customer-facing application
3. Run internal business applications

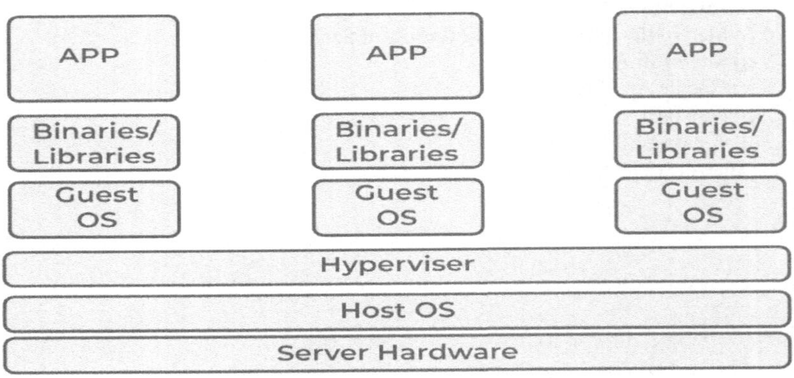

Virtualization

Virtualization

- Host Machine: The machine on which the virtual machine is going to be built is known as Host Machine.
- Guest Machine: The virtual machine is referred to as a Guest Machine.

Work of Virtualization in Cloud Computing

Virtualization has a prominent impact on Cloud Computing. In the case of cloud computing, users store data in the cloud, but with the help of Virtualization, users have the extra benefit of sharing the infrastructure. Cloud Vendors take care of the required physical resources, but these cloud providers charge a huge amount for these services which impacts every user or organization. Virtualization helps Users or Organisations in maintaining those services which are required by a company through external (third-party) people, which helps in reducing costs to the company. This is the way through which Virtualization works in Cloud Computing.

Benefits of Virtualization

- More flexible and efficient allocation of resources.
- Enhance development productivity.
- It lowers the cost of IT infrastructure.
- Remote access and rapid scalability.
- High availability and disaster recovery.
- Pay peruse of the IT infrastructure on demand.
- Enables running multiple operating systems.

Drawback of Virtualization

- High Initial Investment: Clouds have a very high initial investment, but it is also true that it will help in reducing the cost of companies.
- Learning New Infrastructure: As the companies shifted from Servers to Cloud, it requires highly skilled staff who have skills to work with the cloud easily, and for this, you have to hire new staff or provide training to current staff.
- Risk of Data: Hosting data on third-party resources can lead to putting the data at risk, it has the chance of getting attacked by any hacker or cracker very easily.

Types of Virtualization:

1. Hardware Virtualization.
2. Operating system Virtualization.
3. Server Virtualization.
4. Storage Virtualization.

1) Hardware Virtualization:

When the virtual machine software or virtual machine manager *(VMM) is directly installed on the hardware system* is known as hardware virtualization.

The main job of hypervisor is to control and monitoring the processor, memory and other hardware resources.

After virtualization of hardware system we can install different operating system on it and run different applications on those OS.

Usage:

Hardware virtualization is mainly done for the server platforms, because controlling virtual machines is much easier than controlling a physical server.

2) Operating System Virtualization:

When the virtual machine software or virtual machine manager *(VMM) is installed on the Host operating system* instead of directly on the hardware system is known as operating system virtualization.

Usage:

Operating System Virtualization is mainly used for testing the applications on different platforms of OS.

3) Server Virtualization:

When the virtual machine software or virtual machine manager *(VMM) is directly installed on the Server system* is known as server virtualization.

Usage:

Server virtualization is done because a single physical server can be divided into multiple servers on the demand basis and for balancing the load.

4) Storage Virtualization:

Storage virtualization is the *process of grouping the physical storage from multiple network storage devices so that it looks like a single storage device.*

Storage virtualization is also implemented by using software applications.

Virtualization reference model:-

The virtualization reference model in cloud computing is a framework that outlines the different layers and components involved in virtualization. It helps in understanding how virtual resources are created, managed, and utilized within a cloud environment.

At the base layer, the model for the hardware is declared or manifested on terms of an architecture i.e. Instruction Set Architecture (ISA).

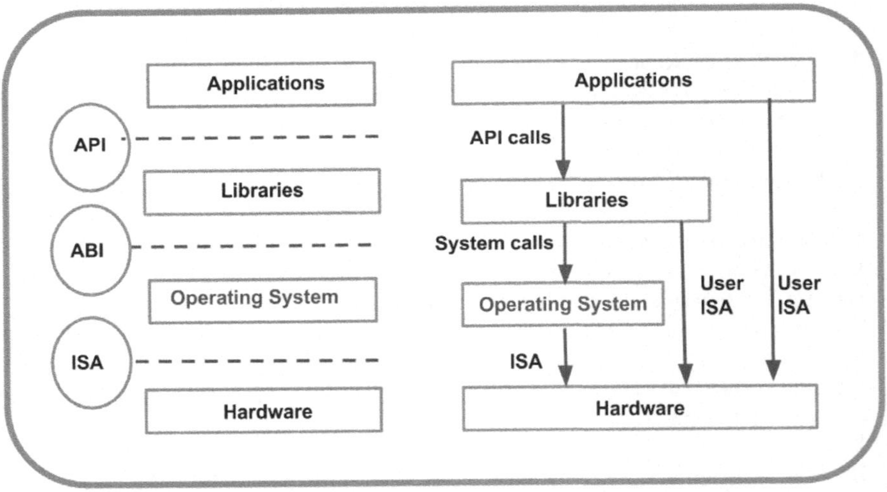

Figure- A machine reference model

Instruction Set Architecture (ISA) defines the instruction set for the processor, registers, memory, and interrupt management. It is an interface between software and hardware and It is mandatory for the operating system (OS) developer (system ISA) developers of applications who directly manages core hardware (user ISA). The operating system layer is separated by the application binary interface (ABI) from the application and libraries, which are managed by operating system.

Application Binary Interface (ABI) covers facts such as low-level data types and call conventions and it also defines a format for many programs. Mainly, system calls are defined at this level. Moreover, this type of interface enables portability of various applications and libraries across OS which employ the same ABI. Application programming interface (API) is represented by the highest level of abstraction. This API interfaces applications to libraries and/or the core OS. For an action is to be performed in the application level API, ABI and the two which are responsible to make it done. Mainly, CPU runs on two privilege levels:

1. User Mode: In this mode, memory access is restricted up to some limit whereas access to peripherals is denied.
2. Kernel Mode: In this mode, CPU has instructions which manage memory and how to be accessed and it also has instructions which enable access of the peripherals like disks and network cards. From one running program to another running program, CPU switches automatically. The expansions and applications of computing system are simplified by this layered approach. Application of multitasking and co-existence of multiple executing is simplified by this layered approach.

The first can be made within privileged and non-privileged instructions. Those instructions which can be used with interrupting with another task are known as Non- privileged instruction. They are also called so because shared resources are not accessed. Ex- contains all the fixed points, floating and arithmetic instructions. The instructions which are executed under particular restrictions and which are frequently used for sensitive operations (which expose behavior-sensitive or modify control sensitive) are known as *privileged instructions*.

Differentiate :- Hypervisor Type 1 vs. Type 2 in Tabular Form

Criteria	Type 1 hypervisor	Type 2 hypervisor
AKA	Bare-metal or Native	Hosted
Definition	Runs directly on the system with VMs running on them	Runs on a conventional Operating System
Virtualization	Hardware Virtualization	OS Virtualization
Operation	Guest OS and applications run on the hypervisor	Runs as an application on the host OS
Scalability	Better Scalability	Not so much, because of its reliance on the underlying OS.
Setup/Installation	Simple, as long as you have the necessary hardware support	Lot simpler setup, as you already have an Operating System.
System Independence	Has direct access to hardware along with virtual machines it hosts	Are not allowed to directly access the host hardware and its resources
Speed	Faster	Slower because of the system's dependency
Performance	Higher-performance as there's no middle layer	Comparatively has reduced performance rate as it runs with extra overhead
Security	More Secure	Less Secure, as any problem in the base operating system affects the entire system including the protected Hypervisor
Examples	• VMware ESXi • Microsoft Hyper-V • Citrix XenServer	• VMware Workstation Player • Microsoft Virtual PC • Sun's VirtualBox

What is Storage Virtualization in Cloud Computing?

Storage **virtualization in Cloud Computing** is nothing but the sharing of physical storage into multiple storage devices which further appears to be a single storage device. It can be also called as a group of an available storage device which simply manages from a central console. This virtualization provides numerous benefits such as easy backup, achieving, and recovery of the data.

Types of Storage Virtualization

Here, we are going to list down all the storage virtualization in Cloud Computing;

- Hardware Assisted Virtualization
- Kernel Level Virtualization
- Hypervisor Virtualization
- Para-Virtualization
- Full Virtualization

i. Hardware Assisted Virtualization

This type of virtualization requires hardware support. It is similar to full Para-virtualization. Here, the unmodified OS can run as **hardware** support for virtualization and we can also use to handle hardware access requests and protect operations.

ii. Kernel Level Virtualization

It runs a separate version of the Linux Kernel. Kernel level allows running multiple servers in a single host. It uses a device driver to communicate between main Linux Kernel and the virtual machine. This virtualization is a special form of **Server Virtualization**.

iii. Hypervisor Virtualization

A hypervisor is a layer between the **Operating system** and hardware. With the help of hypervisor multiple operating systems can work. Moreover, it **provides features** and necessary services which help OS to work properly.

iv. Para-Virtualization

It is based on hypervisor which handles emulation and trapping of software. Here, the guest operating system is modified before installing it to any further machine. The modified system communicates directly with the hypervisor and improves the performance.

v. Full Virtualization

This virtualization is similar to Para-Virtualization. In this, the hypervisor traps the machine operations which is used by theoperating system to perform the operations. After trapping the operations, it emulates in particular software and the status codes returned.

Advantages of Storage Virtualization

1. Data is stored in the more convenient locations away from the specific host. In the case of a host failure, the data is not compromised necessarily.
2. The storage devices can perform advanced functions like replication, reduplication, and disaster recovery functionality.

3. By doing abstraction of the storage level, IT operations become more flexible in how storage is provided, partitioned, and protected.

Multitenancy in Cloud computing

Multitenancy is a type of software architecture where a single software instance can serve multiple distinct user groups. It means that multiple customers of cloud vendors are using the same computing resources. As they are sharing the same computing resources but the data of each Cloud customer is kept separate and secure. It is a very important concept of Cloud Computing.
Multitenancy is also a shared host where the same resources are divided among different customers in cloud computing.

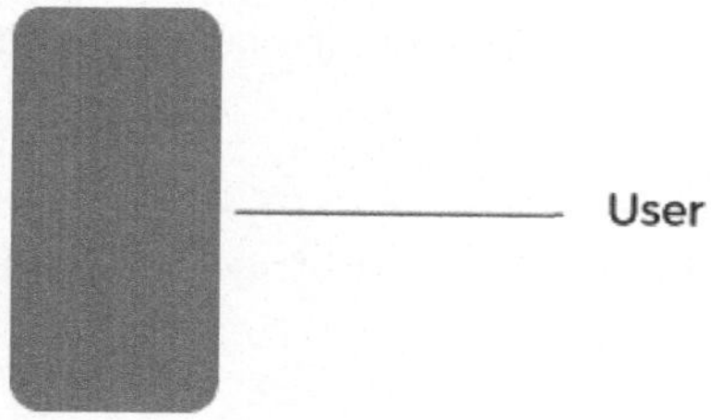

Single tenant

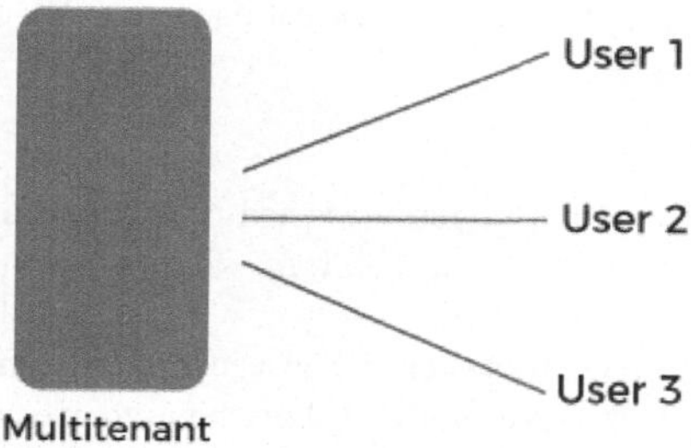

Multitenant

For Example :
The example of multitenancy is the same as working of Bank. Multiple people can store money in the same Bank. But every customer asset is different. One customer cannot access the other customer's money and account, and different customers are not aware of each other's account balance and details, etc.

Advantages of Multitenancy :

- The use of Available resources is maximized by sharing resources.
- Customer's Cost of Physical Hardware System is reduced, and it reduces the usage of physical devices and thus power consumption and cooling cost savings.
- Save Vendor's cost as it becomes difficult for a cloud vendor to provide separate Physical Services to each individual.

Disadvantages of Multitenancy :

- Data is stored in third-party services, which reduces our data security and puts it into vulnerable conditions.
- Unauthorized access will cause damage to data.

Each tenant's data is not accessible to all other tenants within the cloud infrastructure and can only be accessed with the permission of the cloud provider.

Advantages of Multitenancy:

- Use of Available resources is maximized by sharing resources.
- Customer's Cost of Physical Hardware System is reduces.
- It reduce usage of physical devices and thus power consumption and cooling cost save.
- Save Vendor's cost as it become difficult for cloud vendor to provide separate Physical Services to each individual.
- Provides isolation to user while maximizing resource utilization.

Disadvantages of Multitenancy:

- As data is stored in third party services , this reduces security of our data and put it into vulnerable condition .
- Unauthorized access will cause damage of data.
- Possibility of competition for system resources.
- It has single point of failure since there is only one instance of resource, clients face loss of service in such cases.

What is a hypervisor

A hypervisor, also known as a virtual machine monitor or VMM. The hypervisor is a piece of software that allows us to build and run virtual machines which are abbreviated as VMs.
A hypervisor allows a single host computer to support multiple virtual machines (VMs) by sharing resources including memory and processing.

What is the use of a hypervisor?

Hypervisors allow the use of more of a system's available resources and provide greater IT versatility because the guest VMs are independent of the host hardware which is one of the major benefits of the Hypervisor.
In other words, this implies that they can be quickly switched between servers. Since a hypervisor with the help of its special feature, it allows several virtual machines to operate on a single physical server. So, it helps us to reduce:

- The Space efficiency
- The Energy uses
- The Maintenance requirements of the server.

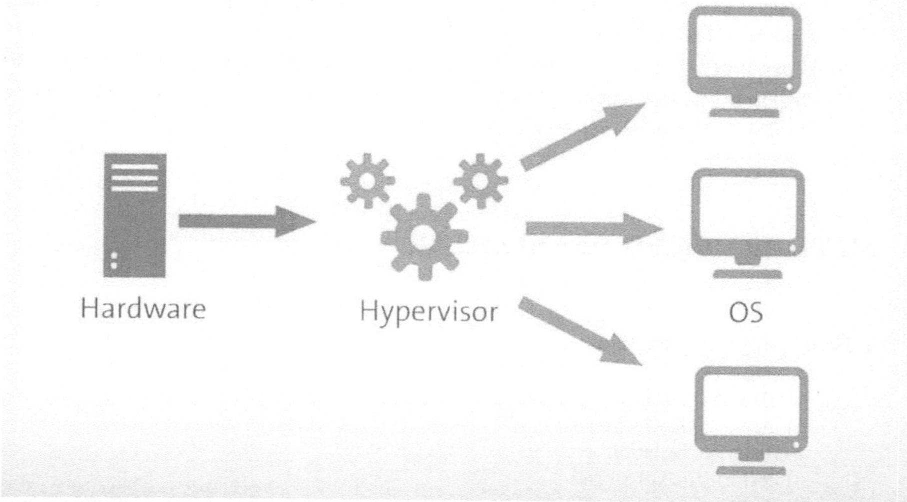

The Type 1 hypervisor

The native or bare metal hypervisor, the Type 1 hypervisor is known by both names.

It replaces the host operating system, and the hypervisor schedules VM services directly to the hardware.

The type 1 hypervisor is very much commonly used in the enterprise data center or other server-based environments.

It includes KVM, Microsoft Hyper-V, and VMware vSphere. If we are running the updated version of the hypervisor then we must have already got the KVM integrated into the Linux kernel in 2007.

The Type 2 hypervisor

It is also known as a hosted hypervisor, The type 2 hypervisor is a software layer or framework that runs on a traditional operating system.

It operates by separating the guest and host operating systems. The host operating system schedules VM services, which are then executed on the hardware.

Individual users who wish to operate multiple operating systems on a personal computer should use a form 2 hypervisor.

This type of hypervisor also includes the virtual machines with it.

Benefits of hypervisors

Using a hypervisor to host several virtual machines has many advantages:

- **Speed:** The hypervisors allow virtual machines to be built instantly unlike bare-metal servers. This makes provisioning resources for complex workloads much simpler.
- **Efficiency:** Hypervisors that run multiple virtual machines on the resources of a single physical machine often allow for more effective use of a single physical server.
- **Flexibility:** Since the hypervisor distinguishes the OS from the underlying hardware, the program no longer relies on particular hardware devices or drivers, bare-metal

hypervisors enable operating systems and their related applications to operate on a variety of hardware types.

- **Portability:** Multiple operating systems can run on the same physical server thanks to hypervisors (host machine). The hypervisor's virtual machines are portable because they are separate from the physical computer.

SAMPLE MCQ QUESTIONS AND ANSWER

1. Issues with Virtualization

1. **Which of the following is a major issue in virtualization?**
   a) Increased hardware cost
   b) Resource isolation
   c) Performance overhead
   d) Reduced resource utilization
   Answer: c) Performance overhead
2. **Security challenges in virtualization are mainly due to:**
   a) Hardware failure
   b) Hypervisor vulnerabilities
   c) RAM shortage
   d) Limited bandwidth
   Answer: b) Hypervisor vulnerabilities
3. **Which issue occurs when multiple VMs try to use the same physical resource?**
   a) Network throttling
   b) Resource contention
   c) Load balancing
   d) Data replication
   Answer: b) Resource contention

---

2. Virtualization Technologies and Architectures

4. **Which of the following is NOT a type of virtualization technology?**
   a) Server virtualization
   b) Application virtualization
   c) BIOS virtualization
   d) Storage virtualization
   Answer: c) BIOS virtualization
5. **In full virtualization, which component emulates the entire hardware?**
   a) Operating System
   b) Hypervisor
   c) BIOS
   d) Kernel
   Answer: b) Hypervisor

6. **Which virtualization architecture runs directly on hardware without a host OS?**
a) Hosted virtualization
b) Bare-metal virtualization
c) Container-based virtualization
d) Desktop virtualization
Answer: b) Bare-metal virtualization

---

3. Internals of Virtual Machine Monitors (VMM)/Hypervisors

7. **A hypervisor is also known as:**
a) Virtual kernel
b) Virtual host
c) Virtual Machine Monitor
d) Load balancer
Answer: c) Virtual Machine Monitor
8. **Which hypervisor type runs on top of a host operating system?**
a) Type 1
b) Type 2
c) Cloud Hypervisor
d) Edge Hypervisor
Answer: b) Type 2
9. **Which of the following is an example of a Type 1 hypervisor?**
a) Oracle VirtualBox
b) VMware Workstation
c) VMware ESXi
d) QEMU
Answer: c) VMware ESXi
10. **Which component is responsible for managing guest operating systems in a virtual environment?**
a) Host OS
b) Middleware
c) Hypervisor
d) Cloud API
Answer: c) Hypervisor

---

4. Virtualization of Data Centers and Multi-Tenancy Issues

11. **Which of the following is NOT a benefit of data center virtualization?**
a) Reduced energy usage
b) Improved scalability
c) Increased hardware maintenance
d) Better resource utilization
Answer: c) Increased hardware maintenance
12. **Multi-tenancy in cloud computing refers to:**
a) One user using multiple clouds
b) One tenant using all physical servers

c) Multiple users sharing the same cloud infrastructure
d) Dedicated hardware for each tenant
Answer: c) Multiple users sharing the same cloud infrastructure

13. **Which is a risk in a multi-tenant environment?**
a) Faster resource provisioning
b) Lower operational cost
c) Data leakage between tenants
d) Increased hardware cost
Answer: c) Data leakage between tenants

---

5. Storage Virtualization

14. **Storage virtualization is the process of:**
a) Converting cloud data into physical format
b) Hiding the complexity of physical storage
c) Replacing hard disks with SSDs
d) Creating VMs for backup
Answer: b) Hiding the complexity of physical storage
15. **Which of the following is a benefit of storage virtualization?**
a) Reduced storage capacity
b) Increased hardware dependency
c) Centralized management
d) Lower network speed
Answer: c) Centralized management
16. **Which component pools physical storage from multiple devices into one logical unit?**
a) RAID Controller
b) SAN Switch
c) Storage Hypervisor
d) Load Balancer
Answer: c) Storage Hypervisor

---

6. Challenges in Virtualization

17. **Which of the following is a key challenge in virtualization?**
a) Hardware cost
b) Compatibility with legacy systems
c) Lower security
d) Limited virtualization tools
Answer: b) Compatibility with legacy systems
18. **Which challenge affects performance in virtualized environments?**
a) Load balancing
b) Virtual machine sprawl
c) Backup and restore
d) Monitoring tools
Answer: b) Virtual machine sprawl

7. Types of Storage Virtualization

19. **In block-level storage virtualization, data is accessed in:**
    a) Files
    b) Bytes
    c) Blocks
    d) Packets
    Answer: c) Blocks
20. **File-level storage virtualization is used mainly in:**
    a) SAN
    b) NAS
    c) RAID 0
    d) SSD
    Answer: b) NAS
21. **Which of the following types of storage virtualization appears as a single storage device to users?**
    a) File-level only
    b) Block-level only
    c) Both block and file-level
    d) None of the above
    Answer: c) Both block and file-level
22. **Which type of storage virtualization uses logical unit numbers (LUNs)?**
    a) File-level
    b) Block-level
    c) Object-based
    d) Volume-based
    Answer: b) Block-level

Unit No. 3 IMPLEMENTATION CLOUD COMPUTING SYSTEM

Cloud Computing Systems

1. Amazon EC2 (Elastic Compute Cloud) and S3 (Simple Storage Service)

- Amazon EC2:
  - A scalable compute service that allows users to run virtual servers (instances) in the cloud.
  - Key Features:
    - Pay-per-use pricing (on-demand, reserved, or spot instances).
    - Automatic scaling and load balancing with Elastic Load Balancer (ELB).
    - Security via AWS Identity and Access Management (IAM).
    - Integration with other AWS services like RDS, S3, and VPC.
  - Use Cases: Hosting websites, running applications, batch processing, and big data analytics.
- Amazon S3:
  - Object storage service for storing and retrieving any amount of data at any time.
  - Key Features:
    - Highly scalable, durable, and secure.
    - Supports features like versioning, lifecycle policies, and cross-region replication.
    - Integrates with services like AWS Lambda (for serverless functions) and Glacier (for archival).
  - Use Cases: Storing backups, web hosting, big data analytics, and disaster recovery.

2. Google App Engine

- Google App Engine (GAE):
  - A fully managed platform for building and deploying web applications.
  - Key Features:
    - PaaS (Platform as a Service) for rapid deployment of apps.
    - Supports languages like Python, Java, PHP, Go, and Node.js.
    - Automatic scaling depending on traffic and load.
    - Integrates with Google Cloud Storage, Google Cloud SQL, and BigQuery.
  - Use Cases: Developing and hosting web and mobile apps without worrying about the underlying infrastructure.

3. Microsoft Azure

- Microsoft Azure:
  - A cloud platform offering a wide range of services including IaaS, PaaS, and SaaS.
  - Key Features:
    - Azure Compute: Virtual Machines (VMs), Azure App Services, Azure Functions (serverless computing).

        - Azure Storage: Blob Storage, Table Storage, File Storage, Queue Storage.
        - Azure Networking: Virtual Network (VNet), Load Balancer, VPN Gateway.
        - Azure Services: AI & machine learning (Azure ML), Analytics (Azure Synapse), and IoT services (Azure IoT Hub).
    - Use Cases: Hosting websites, data analytics, disaster recovery, and hybrid cloud solutions.

Private/Hybrid Cloud Using Open Source Tools

- Private Cloud:
    - A private cloud is a cloud computing model dedicated to a single organization, providing more control over data and infrastructure.
    - Key Open Source Tools for Private Cloud:
        - OpenStack: A widely-used open-source cloud platform for building private and hybrid clouds. It consists of components like Nova (Compute), Swift (Storage), and Neutron (Networking).
        - CloudStack: Another open-source platform for deploying and managing large-scale cloud services.
        - Eucalyptus: An open-source cloud platform that supports hybrid clouds with AWS-compatible APIs.
    - Benefits: Full control over hardware, security, and customization of services.
- Hybrid Cloud:
    - Hybrid cloud integrates on-premise private clouds with public clouds (like AWS, Azure, or Google Cloud) to enable seamless data and application portability.
    - Open Source Tools for Hybrid Cloud:
        - OpenStack with Hybrid Extensions: Used to extend private cloud infrastructures to public clouds.
        - VMware Cloud Foundation: Combines virtualization and hybrid cloud management tools to connect private clouds with public cloud services.
        - Kubernetes: Manages containerized applications and can span hybrid cloud environments, automating deployment and scaling.

Deployment of Web Services in Cloud Architecture

- Web Services in Cloud:
    - Web services allow applications to communicate with each other over a network. In the cloud, web services are typically deployed using APIs (REST, SOAP).
    - Deployment Options:
        - Inside the Cloud: Deploy web services on cloud-based virtual machines (like AWS EC2, Azure VMs).

        - Outside the Cloud: Expose cloud-hosted web services to external clients, such as mobile apps or external systems, using public IPs and secure protocols (SSL/TLS).
        - Serverless Deployment: Using cloud functions (e.g., AWS Lambda, Google Cloud Functions) to run code in response to HTTP requests without managing the underlying infrastructure.
- Cloud API Management:
    - API Gateways like AWS API Gateway or Azure API Management help manage, throttle, and secure web service APIs.

Map Reduce and its Extensions to Cloud Computing

- Map Reduce:
    - A programming model for processing and generating large datasets in parallel across distributed clusters.
    - Map Reduce Steps:
        - Map: Breaks down the task into smaller chunks and processes them in parallel.
        - Reduce: Aggregates the results of the map tasks to produce the final output.
    - Advantages:
        - Scalability: Handles large datasets effectively across many machines.
        - Fault Tolerance: If a node fails, tasks are reassigned to other nodes.
- Extensions of Map Reduce in Cloud:
    - Cloud-Specific Implementations:
        - Amazon EMR (Elastic Map Reduce): Managed service to process vast amounts of data with Hadoop and Spark.
        - Google Cloud Dataproc: Managed Spark and Hadoop clusters.
        - Microsoft Azure HDInsight: Cloud service that supports Hadoop, Spark, and other big data frameworks.
- Apache Hadoop:
    - An open-source framework for processing large datasets using MapReduce, typically running on a cluster of machines.
    - Key Components:
        - HDFS (Hadoop Distributed File System): Distributed storage system designed to store vast amounts of data across multiple nodes.
        - YARN (Yet Another Resource Negotiator): Manages resources in the Hadoop cluster and schedules jobs.
        - MapReduce: Data processing framework for parallel computation.
- GFS (Google File System):
    - A scalable distributed file system used by Google for storing large datasets across multiple servers.
    - Differences between HDFS and GFS:

- Both provide fault-tolerant, distributed storage, but HDFS is designed to run on commodity hardware, whereas GFS was designed for use in Google's internal systems.
- HDFS supports block replication to ensure data redundancy, while GFS does not replicate data as often but provides a high throughput for large files.

Key Concepts for Cloud Implementation

1. Scalability: Cloud services like EC2 and Google App Engine provide automatic scaling, ensuring that applications can handle varying levels of demand without manual intervention.
2. Cost Efficiency: Cloud services charge on a pay-as-you-go basis, allowing businesses to pay only for the resources they use. For example, AWS EC2 instances can be scaled up or down based on the current load, optimizing costs.
3. Security: Cloud platforms provide tools for securing applications, data, and infrastructure, including encryption, identity management, and access control (IAM in AWS, RBAC in Azure).
4. Reliability and Availability: Cloud services like S3 and Azure Storage offer redundancy and failover to ensure high availability and data durability. Services like AWS Elastic Load Balancer and Azure Load Balancer distribute traffic across multiple instances to avoid downtime.

Key Takeaways:

- Amazon EC2 and S3 are core services that allow organizations to rent computing power and store data in the cloud.
- Google App Engine offers a fully managed platform for deploying apps without managing infrastructure.
- Microsoft Azure provides a comprehensive cloud platform with a wide array of services for compute, storage, and networking.
- Private and Hybrid Clouds: Tools like OpenStack, CloudStack, and Kubernetes enable building private and hybrid clouds, combining the benefits of both on-premises and public cloud resources.
- Web Services in Cloud: Cloud platforms provide various ways to deploy, manage, and secure web services both inside and outside the cloud.
- MapReduce and Big Data: Cloud providers offer managed services (e.g., AWS EMR, Google Dataproc) for big data processing using the MapReduce paradigm, with Hadoop and HDFS/GFS as core technologies.

The concept of Map reduce withneat sketch

MapReduce is a programming model designed for processing large datasets in a distributed manner. It is widely used in **big data processing** and is the foundation for frameworks like **Hadoop**.

The MapReduce model divides the computation into two primary tasks: **Map** and **Reduce**.

1. Map Phase:

In the **Map** phase, the input data is divided into smaller subproblems (key-value pairs). These subproblems are processed in parallel by multiple **map tasks** running on different nodes in the distributed system. Each map task processes a chunk of data and outputs intermediate key-value pairs.

- **Input**: The input data is typically a large set of key-value pairs (e.g., a document).
- **Map Function**: This function reads the input, processes it, and generates intermediate key-value pairs.

For example, consider the task of counting word frequencies in a large document:

- **Input Data**: A set of documents.
- **Map Function**: For each document, the function processes the text and emits intermediate key-value pairs where the key is a word, and the value is the number 1 (indicating the word appeared once).

Example:

- Input: "hello world"
- Output: ("hello", 1), ("world", 1)

2. Shuffle and Sort Phase:

After the map tasks are done, the framework moves on to the **Shuffle and Sort** phase. In this phase, the **key-value pairs** produced by the Map tasks are grouped by key. This phase is handled automatically by the MapReduce framework.

- The system sorts the intermediate key-value pairs by key.
- It groups all values associated with the same key together, so they can be processed together in the next phase.

For example:

- After **Map** step:
    - "hello" → 1
    - "world" → 1
    - "hello" → 1
- After **Shuffle and Sort**:
    - ("hello", [1, 1])
    - ("world", [1])

3. Reduce Phase:

In the **Reduce** phase, each **reducer** receives a key and a list of values associated with that key. The **reduce function** aggregates the values (e.g., summing them) to produce a final result.

For the word count example:

- **Reducer** receives the key "hello" and values [1, 1].
- It sums the values: 1 + 1 = 2.

Output: The final result is a collection of key-value pairs where the key is the word, and the value is the total count of occurrences of that word.

Example:

- Input to the **Reduce** function: ("hello", [1, 1])
- Output: ("hello", 2)

After reducing, you get the final word count result:

- ("hello", 2)

- ("world", 1)

4. Final Output:

The output is the final result after all reduce tasks are completed. This can be written to a distributed file system or database.

MapReduce Flow (With Sketch):

1. **Input Data**: The data is divided into chunks (usually splits of files).
2. **Map Phase**: Each chunk is processed by a mapper that outputs intermediate key-value pairs.
3. **Shuffle and Sort Phase**: The intermediate results are sorted by keys, and grouped together.
4. **Reduce Phase**: The grouped results are processed by reducers, where the aggregation or computation happens.
5. **Final Output**: The reduced results are written to storage.

Neat Sketch of MapReduce:

Here's a simplified flow of the **MapReduce process**:

sql

Copy code

```
    +---------------------+
    |   Input Data      |
    | (Large Dataset)     |
    +---------------------+
            |
            v
  +---------------------+
  |     Mapper        | -----> (Map Phase)
  | (Process Data, Emit |
  | Key-Value Pairs)    |
  +---------------------+
            |
            v
  +---------------------+
  | Shuffle & Sort      | -----> (Shuffle Phase)
  | (Group & Sort Pairs) |
  +---------------------+
            |
            v
  +---------------------+
  |     Reducer       | -----> (Reduce Phase)
  | (Aggregate Results) |
  +---------------------+
            |
            v
   +-------------------+
   |  Final Output   | -----> (Final Result)
```

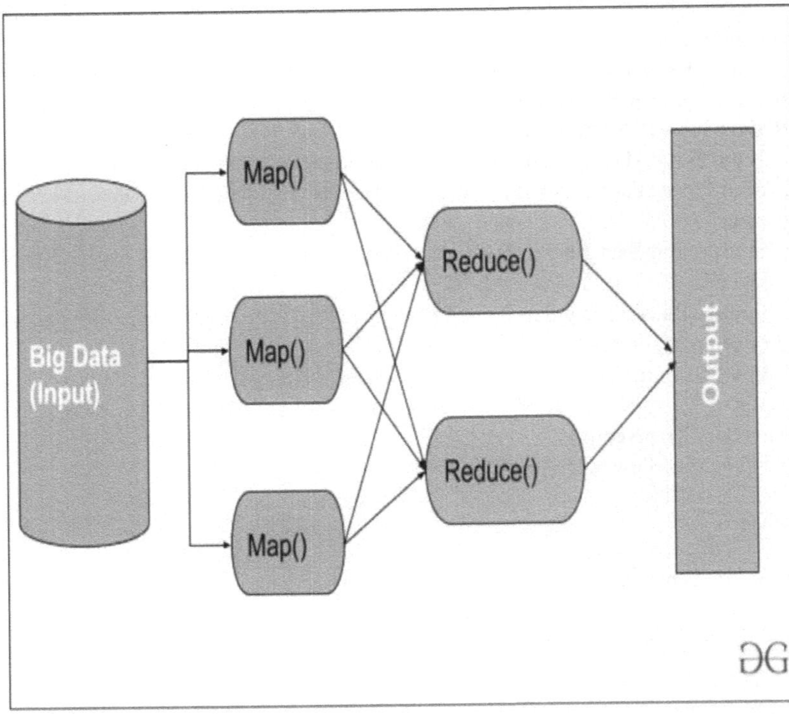

Fig : Map Reduce in Hadoop

Key Concepts in MapReduce:

- **Map Function**: Applies a transformation to each input record and produces intermediate results (key-value pairs).
- **Shuffle & Sort**: The system groups the intermediate data by key and ensures that all values for a key are sent to the same reducer.
- **Reduce Function**: Aggregates the values associated with a key to produce the final result.
- **Fault Tolerance**: If a node fails during the process, tasks are rescheduled on other available nodes.
- **Parallelism**: The power of MapReduce lies in parallelizing the task execution, where mappers and reducers run independently on different nodes in a cluster.

Use Cases:

- **Word Count**: Counting the frequency of words in large text files.
- **Log Analysis**: Processing server logs to generate insights or detect anomalies.
- **Data Mining**: Large-scale data processing tasks like clustering, classification, and association rule mining.

Advantages of MapReduce:

- **Scalability**: Can process massive amounts of data by distributing the work across many nodes.
- **Fault Tolerance**: If a task fails, it can be retried on another node.
- **Simplicity**: It abstracts the complexity of parallel and distributed computing from the programmer.
- **Cost-Efficient**: Works well with large, distributed clusters, often running on commodity hardware.

Components of Hadoop and its advantages

Components of Hadoop

Hadoop Distributed File System (HDFS):

- **Purpose**: Stores large datasets across multiple machines.
- **Key Components**:
    - **NameNode**: Manages file metadata and block locations.
    - **DataNode**: Stores actual data blocks.
- **Features**: Data is split into blocks and replicated for fault tolerance.

2. **MapReduce**:
    - **Purpose**: A programming model for parallel data processing.
    - **Key Components**:
        - **JobTracker**: Manages job execution.
        - **TaskTracker**: Executes tasks on nodes.
    - **Flow**: Data is processed in parallel using **Map** and **Reduce** functions.
3. **YARN (Yet Another Resource Negotiator)**:
    - **Purpose**: Manages and schedules resources across the Hadoop cluster.
    - **Key Components**:
        - **ResourceManager**: Manages resources across the cluster.
        - **NodeManager**: Manages resources on each node.
        - **ApplicationMaster**: Manages application execution.
4. **Hadoop Common**:
    - **Purpose**: Provides libraries and utilities for Hadoop components.
    - **Key Features**: Includes file system support, configuration management, and data serialization.
5. **Hadoop Ecosystem**:
    - **Tools/Technologies**: Hive (SQL-like querying), Pig (data processing), HBase (NoSQL database), Spark (in-memory processing), Flume, Sqoop, Oozie, Mahout (machine learning), etc.

Advantages of Hadoop (Short Answer)

1. **Scalability**: Can scale from a single server to thousands of nodes.
2. **Cost-Effective**: Uses commodity hardware and open-source software.

3. **Fault Tolerance**: Data is replicated across nodes to ensure availability even in case of failures.
4. **Flexibility**: Can handle both structured and unstructured data.
5. **Parallel Processing**: Enables faster processing by distributing tasks across multiple nodes.
6. **High Availability**: Data is replicated to ensure continuous access.
7. **Performance**: Large datasets are processed faster through parallel execution.
8. **Open Source**: Reduces software costs and is actively maintained by the community.
9. **Integration**: Integrates with other tools like Hive, Pig, and Spark for diverse processing tasks.

Hadoop is a powerful, scalable, and cost-effective solution for big data storage and processing.

What is storage virtualization? Explain different types of storage virtualization.

Storage Virtualization

Storage Virtualization is the process of abstracting physical storage resources into a unified, logical view to simplify storage management, improve efficiency, and optimize resource utilization. It allows for easier management of storage across multiple devices and systems, making it more flexible and scalable.

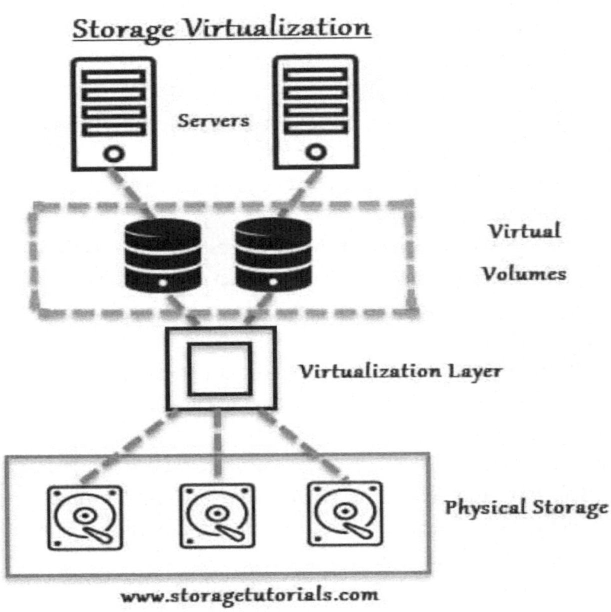

Types of Storage Virtualization

1. **Block-Level Virtualization**:

  - Abstracts storage at the block level, presenting storage as raw blocks across multiple devices.
  - **Used in**: Storage Area Networks (SANs).
  - **Advantages**: Flexibility, scalability, and efficient storage management.
2. **File-Level Virtualization**:
   - Virtualizes storage at the file system level, abstracting data into files and directories.
   - **Used in**: Network Attached Storage (NAS).
   - **Advantages**: Simplifies file management, easier data access, and backup.
3. **Object-Level Virtualization**:
   - Abstracts storage as objects with unique identifiers, usually in cloud environments.
   - **Used in**: Cloud storage (e.g., Amazon S3).
   - **Advantages**: Highly scalable, efficient for unstructured data storage.
4. **Hybrid Storage Virtualization**:
   - Combines block and file virtualization for flexible and efficient storage management.
   - **Used in**: Software-Defined Storage (SDS).
   - **Advantages**: Optimizes storage performance across multiple tiers.
5. **Software-Defined Storage (SDS)**:
   - Virtualizes storage through software, decoupling storage from hardware.
   - **Used in**: SDS platforms (e.g., VMware vSAN).
   - **Advantages**: Hardware independence, centralized management, scalability.

Advantages of Storage Virtualization

- **Increased Efficiency**: Maximizes storage utilization.
- **Simplified Management**: Centralized management of resources.
- **Cost Savings**: Reduces hardware dependency.
- **Scalability**: Easy to expand storage as needed.
- **Flexibility**: Supports diverse storage systems.
- **Data Migration**: Simplifies moving data across environments.

Storage virtualization is essential for managing large and complex storage infrastructures, providing flexibility, scalability, and improved resource utilization.

SAMPLE MCQ QUESTIONS AND ANSWER

1. Amazon EC2 and S3

1. **Amazon EC2 is mainly used for:**
   a) File storage
   b) Computing power
   c) Email service
   d) Database replication
   Answer: b) Computing power
2. **What does EC2 stand for in Amazon EC2?**
   a) Elastic Cloud Control
   b) Elastic Compute Cloud
   c) External Cloud Computing
   d) Elastic Container Cloud
   Answer: b) Elastic Compute Cloud
3. **Amazon S3 is used for:**
   a) Web hosting
   b) File storage
   c) Code execution
   d) Network routing
   Answer: b) File storage
4. **In Amazon S3, data is stored in:**
   a) Buckets
   b) Tables
   c) Folders
   d) Nodes
   Answer: a) Buckets

---

2. Google App Engine

5. **Google App Engine is a:**
   a) IaaS platform
   b) PaaS platform
   c) SaaS tool
   d) Virtualization hypervisor
   Answer: b) PaaS platform
6. **Which programming languages are supported by Google App Engine?**
   a) Python, Java, Go
   b) C++, PHP, Perl
   c) Swift, Kotlin, Dart
   d) Ruby, Rust, Pascal
   Answer: a) Python, Java, Go
7. **Google App Engine automatically handles:**
   a) Virtual machine allocation
   b) Software licensing

c) Application scaling
d) Desktop backup
Answer: c) Application scaling

---

3. Microsoft Azure

8. **Microsoft Azure is a:**
   a) SaaS tool only
   b) Private cloud only
   c) Cloud computing platform and service
   d) Local development environment
   Answer: c) Cloud computing platform and service
9. **Which company owns and operates Microsoft Azure?**
   a) Amazon
   b) Google
   c) Microsoft
   d) IBM
   Answer: c) Microsoft
10. **Which Azure service is used for deploying virtual machines?**
   a) Azure Blob Storage
   b) Azure Compute
   c) Azure Cosmos DB
   d) Azure App Service
   Answer: b) Azure Compute

---

4. Private/Hybrid Cloud using Open Source Tools

11. **Which of the following is an open-source tool used for building a private cloud?**
   a) AWS
   b) Azure
   c) OpenStack
   d) GCP
   Answer: c) OpenStack
12. **Hybrid cloud is a combination of:**
   a) Private cloud and Edge computing
   b) Public cloud and private cloud
   c) On-premises data only
   d) SaaS and IaaS only
   Answer: b) Public cloud and private cloud
13. **Which of these tools can be used to create a hybrid cloud?**
   a) OpenNebula
   b) GitHub
   c) Jenkins
   d) Bitbucket
   Answer: a) OpenNebula

---

5. Deployment of Web Services from Inside/Outside a Cloud Architecture

14. **Deploying a web service inside a cloud means:**
 a) Hosting it on physical hardware only
 b) Hosting it using cloud infrastructure
 c) Hosting via offline mode
 d) Running it through a mobile app only
 Answer: b) Hosting it using cloud infrastructure
15. **Which protocol is commonly used for accessing web services?**
 a) HTTP
 b) SMTP
 c) FTP
 d) DHCP
 Answer: a) HTTP
16. **Deploying web services outside the cloud means:**
 a) Not using any internet
 b) Deploying on on-premises infrastructure
 c) Using container orchestration
 d) Hosting using mobile devices
 Answer: b) Deploying on on-premises infrastructure

---

6. MapReduce and Its Extensions to Cloud Computing

17. **MapReduce is mainly used for:**
 a) Web hosting
 b) File encryption
 c) Large-scale data processing
 d) Memory management
 Answer: c) Large-scale data processing
18. **The two key phases in MapReduce are:**
 a) Shuffle and Load
 b) Sort and Filter
 c) Map and Reduce
 d) Transfer and Replicate
 Answer: c) Map and Reduce
19. **MapReduce was originally developed by:**
 a) Microsoft
 b) Amazon
 c) Google
 d) IBM
 Answer: c) Google

---

7. Hadoop

20. **Hadoop is mainly used for:**
    a) Managing email servers
    b) Distributed storage and processing of big data
    c) Creating spreadsheets
    d) Data encryption
    Answer: b) Distributed storage and processing of big data
21. **Which programming model does Hadoop use?**
    a) Event-driven
    b) Pipeline
    c) MapReduce
    d) Actor model
    Answer: c) MapReduce

---

8. HDFS (Hadoop Distributed File System)

22. **HDFS stands for:**
    a) High-Density File Storage
    b) Hadoop Distributed File System
    c) Hybrid Disk File System
    d) Host Data File Storage
    Answer: b) Hadoop Distributed File System
23. **In HDFS, data is split into blocks and stored:**
    a) Randomly on a hard drive
    b) On a central disk
    c) Across multiple nodes
    d) Only in memory
    Answer: c) Across multiple nodes
24. **What is the default block size in HDFS (pre-Hadoop 2)?**
    a) 32 MB
    b) 64 MB
    c) 128 MB
    d) 256 MB
    Answer: b) 64 MB

---

9. GFS (Google File System)

25. **Google File System (GFS) is designed for:**
    a) Small file storage
    b) Real-time analytics
    c) Large-scale data storage
    d) Web hosting only
    Answer: c) Large-scale data storage
26. **In GFS, files are divided into:**
    a) Chunks

b) Packets
c) Threads
d) Segments
Answer: a) Chunks

27. **The default chunk size in GFS is:**
a) 16 MB
b) 32 MB
c) 64 MB
d) 128 MB
Answer: d) 128 MB

Unit No. 04 BUSINESS CONTINUITY AND RECOVERY

1. Information Availability

- Definition: Information availability refers to the ability of a system to keep data accessible to users whenever needed, with minimal downtime.
- Key Factors:
    - Uptime: Ensuring the system is available and operational.
    - Data Redundancy: Duplicating data across multiple locations or systems to prevent loss.
    - Disaster Recovery Plans: Having clear procedures to recover from system failures or disasters.

---

2. Business Continuity Life Cycle

The business continuity life cycle refers to the process of planning, implementing, and testing the continuity measures that keep an organization operational during a crisis. The cycle generally includes the following phases:

1. Risk Assessment and Business Impact Analysis (BIA): Identifying potential risks, threats, and the impact of disruptions on business functions.
2. Strategy Development: Creating strategies to maintain or quickly restore critical business operations.
3. Plan Development: Developing detailed business continuity and disaster recovery plans (BCP/DRP).
4. Implementation: Executing the strategies and plans, including infrastructure setup, personnel training, and system configuration.
5. Testing and Validation: Regular testing to ensure the plans work under actual crisis scenarios.
6. Maintenance: Continuous updates and revisions to the business continuity and recovery plans.

---

3. Failure Analysis

Failure analysis is the process of identifying the causes of system failure and assessing its impact on the organization. It helps in creating a more resilient IT environment by mitigating risks.

- Types of Failures:
    - Hardware Failures: Disk crashes, server outages, power supply issues.
    - Software Failures: Bugs, corrupted files, application crashes.
    - Human Errors: Incorrect configurations, accidental deletions, mismanagement.
    - Natural Disasters: Earthquakes, floods, fires that damage data centers.
    - Cybersecurity Threats: Malware attacks, ransomware, hacking.
- Impact Assessment:
    - Evaluate the severity of the failure and how it affects business operations (financial losses, reputational damage, legal/regulatory consequences).

---

4. Backup and Recovery

Backup and recovery refer to the processes used to create copies of critical data and ensure that data can be restored in case of failure or data loss.

- Backup Purpose:
  - Data Protection: Prevent data loss due to hardware failure, human error, or disasters.
  - Disaster Recovery: Enable quick recovery of business operations after a failure.
  - Compliance: Meet regulatory requirements for data retention.
- Backup Considerations:
  - Criticality of Data: Prioritize backing up mission-critical and business-critical data.
  - Backup Frequency: Determine how often backups should be taken (daily, weekly, continuous, etc.).
  - Storage Location: Decide whether to store backups on-premises, off-site, or in the cloud.
  - Security: Ensure backups are encrypted and stored securely to prevent unauthorized access.
  - Backup Integrity: Regularly check and verify the integrity of backups to ensure they can be restored when needed.

---

5. Backup Granularity

Granularity refers to the level of detail or scope of data that is backed up.

- Types of Granularity:
  - Full Backup: A complete copy of all selected data (e.g., all files, databases, or systems).
    - Advantages: Fast recovery, simple to manage.
    - Disadvantages: Time-consuming and storage-intensive.
  - Incremental Backup: Only the data that has changed since the last backup (either full or incremental) is backed up.
    - Advantages: Faster and requires less storage space.
    - Disadvantages: Slower recovery, as all previous backups must be restored first.
  - Differential Backup: Backs up the data that has changed since the last full backup.
    - Advantages: Faster than full backups, quicker recovery than incremental backups.
    - Disadvantages: Requires more storage space than incremental backups.

---

6. Recovery Considerations

When planning for recovery, the focus is on restoring operations with minimal downtime and data loss.

- Recovery Time Objective (RTO): The maximum acceptable amount of time to restore operations after an outage.
  - RTO should be determined based on business priorities.

- Recovery Point Objective (RPO): The maximum acceptable amount of data loss in case of an incident, typically measured in minutes or hours.
    - RPO dictates the frequency of backups and the granularity level.
- Backup Methods:
    - Local Backup: Storing backups on local disks or storage systems, offering fast recovery but vulnerable to local disasters.
    - Remote/Off-Site Backup: Storing backups at a different physical location, ensuring protection from site-specific disasters.
    - Cloud Backup: Using cloud services to store backups, offering scalability, remote access, and easy management.
- Backup Process:

1. Backup Data: Regularly perform backups according to the backup strategy.
2. Store Backups: Securely store backups, ensuring they are protected and accessible.
3. Monitor: Continuously monitor the status of backups to ensure they are completed without errors.
4. Restore: When needed, recover data from backups according to the recovery plan.

- Backup and Restore Operations:
    - Backup Operation: Involves scheduling, capturing, and securely storing data copies.
    - Restore Operation: Involves retrieving backed-up data from storage and bringing systems or applications back online.

---

7. Emerging Backup Technologies

1. Data Duplication (Deduplication):
    - Purpose: Reduces storage requirements by eliminating duplicate copies of repeating data. Only unique pieces of data are stored.
    - Advantages: Saves storage space and improves backup efficiency.
2. Off-Site Backup:
    - Purpose: Backing up data to a location separate from the primary data center (e.g., another physical site or cloud storage).
    - Advantages: Protects data from local disasters (fires, floods) and provides a failover location for disaster recovery.
    - Methods:
        - Cloud Backup: Storing backups in a cloud environment for easy access and scalability.
        - Physical Off-Site Storage: Storing backup tapes or hard drives at a secure off-site location.
3. Continuous Data Protection (CDP):
    - Purpose: Provides real-time backup by continuously capturing data changes.
    - Advantages: Minimizes RPO (recovery point objective) and ensures that data can be recovered with minimal loss.
    - Example: Snapshots or replication technologies that maintain a constant backup of live data.
4. Cloud Disaster Recovery:

- Purpose: Using cloud services for data replication, backup, and recovery to ensure fast recovery in case of a disaster.
- Advantages: Scalable, cost-effective, and offers flexibility in disaster recovery planning.

Elaborate Google App Engine along with its benefits

Google App Engine (GAE) -

Google App Engine (GAE) is a Platform-as-a-Service (PaaS) provided by Google Cloud that allows developers to build and deploy applications without managing the underlying infrastructure. It handles scaling, security, load balancing, and server management, enabling developers to focus solely on code.

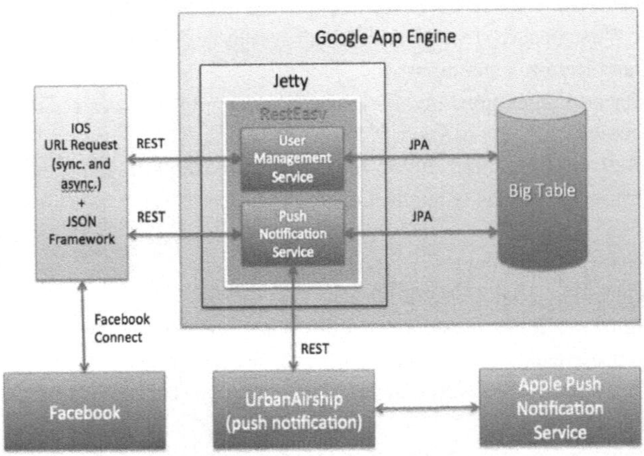

Fig: Google App Engine

Key Features of Google App Engine:

1. Fully Managed Infrastructure: No server management required.
2. Auto-Scaling: Automatically adjusts based on traffic.
3. Supports Multiple Languages: Python, Java, Node.js, Go, PHP, and custom runtimes via Docker.
4. Integrated Developer Tools: Built-in monitoring, debugging, and versioning tools.
5. Global Reach: Deploy applications globally with low-latency access.
6. Security: Includes built-in encryption, identity management, and access control.

Benefits of Google App Engine:

1. No Server Management: Google manages everything related to infrastructure.
2. Scalability: Auto-scaling based on demand.
3. Cost Efficiency: Pay only for the resources used.

4. Faster Development: Simplifies deployment and management, reducing time to market.
5. Global Load Balancing: Traffic is automatically routed to the closest instance.
6. Integrated Monitoring: Uses Google Cloud's Operations Suite for real-time monitoring and debugging.

Use Cases:

- Web Applications: Host scalable websites.
- Mobile Backends: Serve as a backend for mobile apps.
- APIs: Build RESTful APIs.
- Microservices: Develop modular, scalable services.

Explain AWS with its S3 and EC2 services.

Amazon Web Services (AWS) is a cloud platform offering a wide range of computing services, including storage, computing power, and databases. It provides scalable, flexible, and cost-efficient solutions for running applications in the cloud.

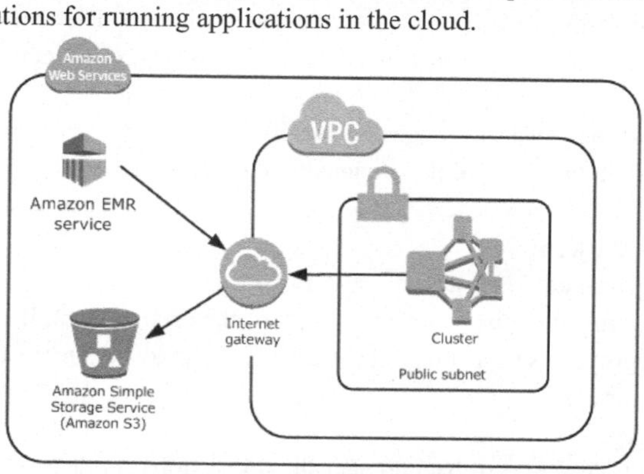

Fig: **AWS with its S3 and EC2 services.**

AWS Services: S3 and EC2

1. Amazon S3 (Simple Storage Service)

- **Purpose**: Object storage service for storing and retrieving any amount of data.
- **Features**:
  - **Scalable**: Unlimited storage.
  - **Durable**: 99.999999999% durability.
  - **Secure**: Encryption and access control.
  - **Flexible**: Different storage classes for cost management.
- **Use Cases**: Data backup, website hosting, media storage, big data storage.

2. Amazon EC2 (Elastic Compute Cloud)

- **Purpose**: Virtual server service that provides resizable compute capacity in the cloud.

- **Features**:
    - **Scalable**: Auto-scaling based on demand.
    - **Customizable**: Choose instance types and operating systems.
    - **Secure**: Integrates with VPC for network isolation.
    - **Cost-Effective**: Pay-as-you-go pricing.
- **Use Cases**: Hosting web applications, big data processing, testing environments, and high-performance computing.

Benefits of AWS (S3 & EC2)

- **Scalability**: S3 and EC2 automatically scale with usage.
- **Cost-Effective**: Pay only for what you use with flexible pricing models.
- **Security**: Built-in encryption, access control, and compliance.
- **Global Reach**: Available across multiple regions and availability zones.
- **Reliability**: High availability with redundancy and fault tolerance.

Define Backup and mention some requirements for backup.

Backup refers to the process of creating copies of data, applications, or entire systems to safeguard against data loss. These copies are stored in a separate location to be used for recovery in case of hardware failure, data corruption, accidental deletion, or disaster events. The primary goal of backup is to ensure that data can be restored to a functional state after loss or damage.

Backups can be made on physical storage devices (like external hard drives) or on remote/cloud services, depending on the needs of the organization or individual.

Requirements for Backup:

1. **Data Integrity and Accuracy**:
    - Backup data must be an exact copy of the original data. It should maintain its integrity, ensuring that files are not corrupted or altered during the backup process.
2. **Redundancy**:
    - Multiple copies of backup data should be stored in different locations (on-site and off-site) to protect against hardware failure, theft, or disaster at a single location. **3-2-1 Rule**: Keep 3 copies of data, 2 on different storage mediums, and 1 off-site.
3. **Scalability**:
    - Backup solutions should be scalable to handle increasing amounts of data as businesses grow. The backup system should allow easy expansion of storage capacity as needed.
4. **Automation**:
    - Backup processes should be automated to ensure they are executed regularly without manual intervention, reducing the risk of human error and ensuring consistency.
5. **Retention Policy**:

  - Clear policies should be in place to determine how long backup copies should be retained. This includes managing versioning and deletion of old backups to optimize storage space.
6. **Security**:
   - Backup data should be encrypted to prevent unauthorized access. Secure storage mechanisms and access controls must be in place to protect backup data from cyber threats or physical theft.
7. **Recovery Speed**:
   - The backup solution must support efficient data recovery. The backup system should allow for fast restoration of data to minimize downtime in case of data loss.
8. **Testing**:
   - Regular testing of backups is essential to ensure that they are valid and can be restored successfully in an emergency. Backup and recovery plans should be tested periodically.
9. **Compliance and Legal Requirements**:
   - Backup solutions should meet any industry-specific regulations regarding data storage, retention, and recovery. For example, healthcare and financial sectors often have strict rules around data retention and privacy (e.g., HIPAA, GDPR).
10. **Version Control**:
    - Backup systems should maintain different versions of data so that older versions can be restored if needed. This helps protect against accidental changes or corruption.
11. **Cost-Effectiveness**:
    - Backup solutions should provide an efficient balance between cost and performance. Organizations should evaluate the cost of backup storage (cloud vs on-premises) and choose an approach that fits their budget while ensuring adequate protection.

SAMPLE MCQ QUESTIONS AND ANSWER

1. Information Availability

1. **What does Information Availability mean?**
   a) Data is readable only by the admin
   b) Data is available only during office hours
   c) Data is accessible when needed, without interruption
   d) Data can be deleted easily
   Answer: c) Data is accessible when needed, without interruption
2. **High availability systems are designed to:**
   a) Reduce data security

b) Minimize downtime
c) Increase backup frequency
d) Allow guest access
Answer: b) Minimize downtime

---

2. Information Lifecycle

3. **Which of the following is NOT a phase in the information lifecycle?**
   a) Creation
   b) Distribution
   c) Deletion
   d) Encryption
   Answer: d) Encryption
4. **Information lifecycle management focuses on:**
   a) Storing data forever
   b) Managing data through its creation to deletion
   c) Encrypting all files
   d) Running only real-time services
   Answer: b) Managing data through its creation to deletion

---

3. Failure Analysis

5. **Failure analysis in IT is used to:**
   a) Reduce software features
   b) Identify causes of system failures
   c) Increase server loads
   d) Replace software updates
   Answer: b) Identify causes of system failures
6. **Which of the following is a common cause of system failure?**
   a) Too many backups
   b) Human error
   c) Using SSDs
   d) Running antivirus
   Answer: b) Human error

---

4. Backup and Recovery – Purpose & Considerations

7. **The main purpose of a backup is to:**
   a) Free up disk space
   b) Secure system access
   c) Create a copy of data to restore if lost
   d) Increase network bandwidth
   Answer: c) Create a copy of data to restore if lost

8. **Which is a consideration when planning a backup strategy?**
   a) Screen resolution
   b) Data importance and frequency of change
   c) Number of users
   d) Print options
   Answer: b) Data importance and frequency of change
9. **Backup granularity refers to:**
   a) The number of backups made
   b) The level of detail or size of data being backed up
   c) The color depth of backup files
   d) The size of the backup disk
   Answer: b) The level of detail or size of data being backed up

5. Recovery Considerations – Methods, Process

10. **Which of the following is a recovery consideration?**
    a) Web design layout
    b) Power consumption
    c) Recovery time objective (RTO)
    d) CPU speed
    Answer: c) Recovery time objective (RTO)
11. **Which backup method stores only data changed since the last full backup?**
    a) Full backup
    b) Incremental backup
    c) Differential backup
    d) Real-time backup
    Answer: b) Incremental backup
12. **Which backup method stores all the data changed since the last full backup, regardless of other backups?**
    a) Differential backup
    b) Full backup
    c) Incremental backup
    d) Snapshot backup
    Answer: a) Differential backup
13. **A full backup means:**
    a) Only the newest files are copied
    b) All selected data is copied entirely
    c) Data is copied in small chunks
    d) Only encrypted files are stored
    Answer: b) All selected data is copied entirely
14. **Which is NOT a valid backup method?**
    a) Incremental
    b) Regressive
    c) Full
    d) Differential
    Answer: b) Regressive

6. Backup and Restore Operations

15. **Which step comes first in the backup and restore process?**
    a) Schedule restore
    b) Data validation
    c) Backup creation
    d) Disk formatting
    Answer: c) Backup creation
16. **Restore operation is used to:**
    a) Create a copy of live data
    b) Recover lost or corrupted data from a backup
    c) Delete old backups
    d) Monitor real-time data
    Answer: b) Recover lost or corrupted data from a backup

---

7. Emerging Technologies – Deduplication, Off-site Backup

17. **Deduplication in backup systems is used to:**
    a) Increase backup time
    b) Save storage space by removing duplicate data
    c) Encrypt backup data
    d) Backup only full images
    Answer: b) Save storage space by removing duplicate data
18. **Which of the following is NOT a benefit of data deduplication?**
    a) Reduced storage needs
    b) Faster backups
    c) Higher redundancy
    d) Lower bandwidth usage
    Answer: c) Higher redundancy
19. **Off-site backup refers to:**
    a) Storing backup copies at the same location
    b) Storing backups in the cloud or another location
    c) Using DVDs for backup
    d) Disabling backup encryption
    Answer: b) Storing backups in the cloud or another location
20. **Which is a key advantage of off-site backup?**
    a) Faster processing speed
    b) Improved physical security and disaster recovery
    c) Requires no Internet
    d) Stores data in temporary memory
    Answer: b) Improved physical security and disaster recovery

Unit No. 05 STORAGE SECURITY AND MANAGEMENT

Storage Security Framework

- Definition: A storage security framework outlines the processes and technologies used to protect storage environments and the data they hold. It ensures data confidentiality, integrity, and availability.

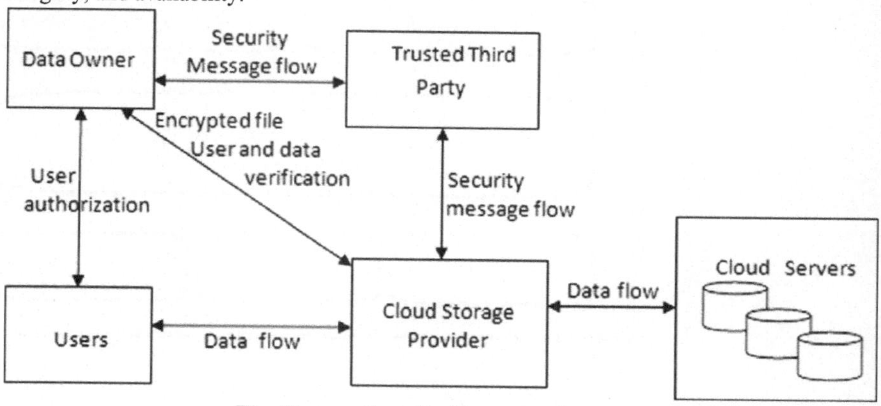

Fig: Storage Security Framework

- **Key Components:**
  - Access Control: Define who can access the data and under what circumstances. Common methods include role-based access control (RBAC), multi-factor authentication (MFA), and least privilege access.
  - Encryption: Protect data both at rest (stored data) and in transit (data being transferred) by encrypting sensitive information.
  - Backup and Disaster Recovery: Ensure regular backup procedures are in place to safeguard against data loss, with disaster recovery plans to restore access in case of failure.
  - Data Integrity: Implement measures to verify that data has not been altered maliciously or by accident.

- **Storage Security Layers:**
  - Physical Security: Protection of the hardware where data is stored (e.g., locking data centers, surveillance).
  - Network Security: Securing the network through which data is transmitted (e.g., firewalls, intrusion detection systems).
  - Application Security: Securing storage applications and databases to protect data during operations.

Securing the Storage Infrastructure

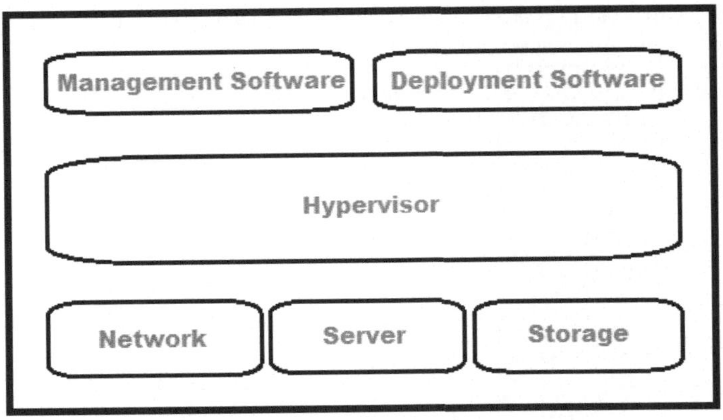

Fig: Cloud Computing Infrastructure

- **Physical Security:**
    - Data centers housing storage systems must be physically secured with restricted access, CCTV surveillance, and security personnel.
- **Network Security:**
    - Use firewalls, Virtual Private Networks (VPNs), and Intrusion Detection Systems (IDS) to secure data in transit between systems and storage devices.
    - Encryption technologies like SSL/TLS or IPsec should be used for network communication to protect data during transmission.
- **Data Encryption:**
    - At Rest: Encrypt sensitive data stored on disk using AES (Advanced Encryption Standard) or other cryptographic algorithms.
    - In Transit: Secure data moving between storage systems and clients using protocols like HTTPS, SFTP, and TLS.
- **Access Control and Authentication:**
    - Implement strong Authentication (e.g., MFA) to ensure only authorized personnel access the storage systems.
    - Use Role-Based Access Control (RBAC) to assign permissions based on the role of the user, reducing the risk of unauthorized data access.
- **Redundancy and High Availability:**
    - Implement RAID (Redundant Array of Independent Disks) or replication to ensure that data remains available even if a hardware failure occurs.

Risk Triad in Storage Management

- The Risk Triad refers to the three core principles of security in storage management:
  - Confidentiality: Ensuring that data is only accessible to authorized users.
  - Integrity: Protecting data from being altered in unauthorized ways.
  - Availability: Ensuring that data is accessible and usable when needed, even in the case of hardware failure or disaster.
- **Risk Management Strategies:**
  - Risk Assessment: Identify potential threats to storage systems (e.g., unauthorized access, data corruption, hardware failure) and assess their impact.
  - Mitigation: Implement technologies and processes to reduce risk, such as encryption, access control, and regular backups.
  - Incident Response: Define clear protocols for detecting, responding to, and recovering from security incidents.

Managing the Storage Infrastructure

- **Storage Infrastructure Components:**
  - Storage Area Network (SAN): A dedicated high-speed network that provides block-level access to storage.
  - Network Attached Storage (NAS): A file-level data storage device that connects to a network and allows users to store and access data over a network.
  - Direct Attached Storage (DAS): Storage that is directly connected to a computer or server without a network.
- **Management Tasks:**
  - Capacity Planning: Ensuring adequate storage space to meet growing data needs.
  - Data Migration: Moving data from one storage system to another for efficiency or redundancy.
  - Backup Management: Regular creation of backup copies and validation of their integrity.
  - Performance Monitoring: Monitoring storage system performance to ensure it is operating efficiently.
- **Tools:**
  - Storage Management Software: Tools like IBM Spectrum Control or NetApp OnCommand that provide central management of storage systems.
  - Automation Tools: Automating backup, migration, and performance monitoring to reduce human error and increase efficiency.

Monitoring the Storage Infrastructure

- **Key Parameters to Monitor:**
  - Storage Utilization: Track how much space is being used and whether it is approaching capacity.

  - Performance Metrics: Monitor IOPS (Input/Output Operations Per Second), throughput, latency, and response times to ensure optimal performance.
  - Health and Status: Regular checks for disk health, temperature, power status, and error logs.
  - Security Events: Monitor for unauthorized access attempts or breaches.
- **Monitoring Tools:**
  - Storage Monitoring Solutions: Use solutions like SolarWinds Storage Manager, Nagios, or Zabbix to monitor storage health and performance.
  - Alerts and Reporting: Set up automated alerts for issues like storage overload, hardware failure, or security breaches.

Key Management Activities and Examples

- **Key Management Activities:**
  - Data Encryption: Implement encryption protocols for data at rest and in transit.
  - Data Backup: Regular backup scheduling to ensure data is recoverable in case of failure.
  - Access Control: Assigning and managing user roles to control who can access or modify stored data.
  - Auditing and Compliance: Regular audits to ensure that security policies are being followed and that the system is compliant with relevant regulations (e.g., GDPR, HIPAA).
- **Examples:**
  - Backup Verification: Regularly test backups to verify that data can be restored without errors.
  - Data Archiving: Moving older, infrequently accessed data to cheaper, slower storage media, while keeping it secure.
  - Encryption Key Rotation: Regularly rotating encryption keys to enhance security.

Storage Management Standards and Industry Trends

- **Storage Management Standards:**
  - ISO/IEC 27001: International standard for information security management, providing guidelines for data protection and risk management.
  - NIST SP 800-53: A set of standards for securing federal information systems in the U.S., often referenced by private organizations as well.
  - GDPR: European Union regulation that mandates data protection and privacy, impacting how storage systems handle sensitive personal data.
  - HIPAA: A U.S. law that requires healthcare organizations to safeguard personal health information (PHI) in storage systems.
- **Industry Trends:**
  - Cloud Storage: Increasing shift towards cloud-based storage solutions (e.g., AWS S3, Microsoft Azure Storage) for scalability, flexibility, and cost-effectiveness.

- Software-Defined Storage (SDS): The use of software to manage storage hardware, providing more flexibility and scalability in storage management.
- Data Deduplication: A technique used to eliminate redundant copies of data, saving storage space and improving backup efficiency.
- Edge Storage: The growing trend of processing and storing data at the "edge" of the network (closer to data sources) for faster access and reduced latency.

Which challenges does the cloud security need to face in day to day life?

Challenges in Cloud Security

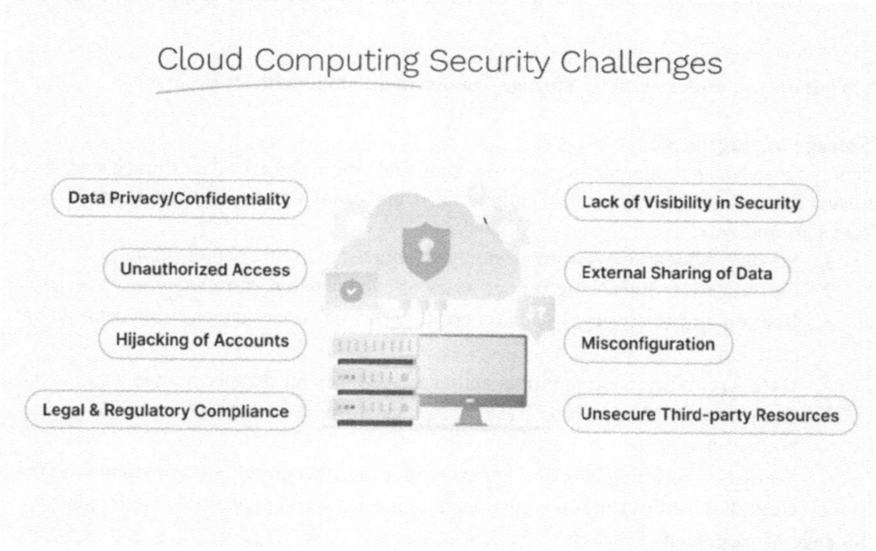

1. **Data Security & Privacy**: Ensuring data protection through encryption, preventing breaches, and managing data residency and sovereignty to comply with regulations like GDPR.
2. **Identity & Access Management (IAM)**: Managing user access, implementing Multi-Factor Authentication (MFA), and enforcing least-privilege access policies.
3. **Shared Responsibility Model**: Understanding the division of security duties between the cloud provider and customer, and avoiding misconfigurations that lead to vulnerabilities.
4. **Insider Threats**: Preventing both malicious and unintentional risks from insiders, including employees and third-party vendors.
5. **Compliance & Regulatory Challenges**: Maintaining compliance with industry regulations (e.g., HIPAA, SOC 2) and ensuring auditability in cloud environments.
6. **Vulnerability Management**: Ensuring regular patching and protection against zero-day vulnerabilities in the cloud infrastructure and services.

7. **Multi-Tenancy Security**: Ensuring secure isolation of data between tenants in shared cloud environments.
8. **Cloud-Specific Attack Vectors**: Protecting against DDoS attacks, securing APIs, and mitigating risks in containers and serverless computing environments.
9. **Cloud Provider Security Posture**: Trusting cloud providers to implement strong security practices and meeting SLAs related to security.
10. **Data Loss & Backup**: Securing backups, ensuring data recovery, and managing retention policies to avoid loss of critical data.
11. **Cloud Storage Security**: Ensuring proper access controls and encryption for cloud storage, and managing data versioning and deletion policies.
12. **Incident Response & Forensics**: Responding to incidents in dynamic cloud environments, collecting evidence, and ensuring proper logging and monitoring.

What do you understand by Storage Management along with its process?

Storage Management:
Storage management refers to the administration and optimization of data storage systems to ensure data is securely stored, efficiently utilized, and easily retrievable when needed.
Key Components:
1. **Storage Allocation**: Assigning storage resources to users or applications.
2. **Optimization**: Enhancing storage space efficiency and performance.
3. **Backup and Recovery**: Regularly creating backup copies and ensuring data can be restored.
4. **Data Archiving**: Storing infrequently accessed data on cheaper storage.
5. **Performance Monitoring**: Tracking storage performance metrics to avoid bottlenecks.
6. **Security**: Protecting data through encryption, access control, and compliance audits.
7. **Compliance**: Ensuring storage practices meet legal and regulatory requirements.

Storage Management Process:
1. **Planning and Provisioning**: Estimating storage needs and allocating resources.
2. **Data Protection**: Implementing backup and disaster recovery solutions.
3. **Data Migration**: Moving data between different storage systems for optimization.
4. **Performance Management**: Monitoring and adjusting storage for optimal speed.
5. **Data Retention and Archiving**: Storing old data efficiently and managing retention policies.
6. **Security Management**: Encrypting data and controlling access to ensure protection.
7. **Decommissioning**: Securely deleting data when storage devices are no longer needed.

Benefits:
1. **Cost Efficiency**: Reducing storage costs through optimization and tiering.
2. **Data Availability**: Ensuring quick access to data and minimizing downtime.
3. **Security and Compliance**: Protecting data and meeting legal requirements.
4. **Scalability**: Easily expanding storage as data grows.
5. **Improved Performance**: Optimizing storage to maintain fast data access.

Storage management ensures that an organization's data is securely stored, efficiently managed, and readily accessible.

Explain Vendor Lock-in Problem in cloud computing along with its Risks

Vendor Lock-in in Cloud Computing

Vendor lock-in occurs when a customer becomes dependent on a specific cloud service provider (CSP) due to proprietary technologies, data formats, or integrations, making it difficult to switch to another provider without significant cost or effort.

Risks of Vendor Lock-in:

1. **Limited Flexibility**: Difficulty adopting new technologies or switching providers.
2. **Cost Increases**: Providers may raise prices, knowing customers are tied to their services.
3. **Reduced Negotiating Power**: Limited ability to negotiate better terms or prices.
4. **Data Portability Issues**: Difficulty moving data due to proprietary formats or services.
5. **Service Dependency**: Reliance on a single provider for all infrastructure, risking service outages or poor performance.
6. **Innovation Stagnation**: Missing out on innovations from competitors.
7. **Compliance & Legal Risks**: Risk of non-compliance if the provider's services change or don't meet regulatory requirements.
8. **High Exit Costs**: Expensive and time-consuming to migrate data and applications to a new provider.

Mitigating Vendor Lock-in Risks:

1. **Use Open Standards and Open Source**: Ensures portability across platforms.
2. **Cloud Agnostic Architecture**: Design applications to work across multiple cloud providers.
3. **Multi-cloud or Hybrid Cloud Strategy**: Distribute workloads across multiple providers to reduce dependency.
4. **Data Portability**: Store data in open, standardized formats.
5. **Negotiate Exit Clauses**: Include exit clauses in contracts for easier migration.

SAMPLE MCQ QUESTIONS AND ANSWER

1. Storage Security Framework

1. **What is the main goal of a storage security framework?**
   a) Reduce data size
   b) Encrypt system logs
   c) Ensure confidentiality, integrity, and availability of data
   d) Improve software licensing
   Answer: c) Ensure confidentiality, integrity, and availability of data

2. **Which of the following is NOT a typical component of storage security?**
   a) Access control
   b) Data encryption
   c) Firewall configuration
   d) Data formatting
   Answer: d) Data formatting
3. **In the storage security framework, data in transit must be protected using:**
   a) Antivirus software
   b) Firewalls
   c) Encryption protocols like SSL/TLS
   d) Disk fragmentation
   Answer: c) Encryption protocols like SSL/TLS

---

2. Securing the Storage Infrastructure

4. **Which one is a method of securing the storage infrastructure?**
   a) Using default passwords
   b) Disabling firewalls
   c) Implementing role-based access control (RBAC)
   d) Reducing disk size
   Answer: c) Implementing role-based access control (RBAC)
5. **Securing storage infrastructure involves:**
   a) Only physical protection
   b) Only software protection
   c) Both physical and logical protection
   d) Only encrypting backup drives
   Answer: c) Both physical and logical protection
6. **Which of these helps prevent unauthorized access to storage systems?**
   a) IP filtering
   b) Open access policies
   c) Guest login
   d) Manual logging
   Answer: a) IP filtering

---

3. Risk Triad

7. **The Risk Triad in storage security includes:**
   a) Cost, time, performance
   b) Confidentiality, integrity, availability
   c) Storage, bandwidth, CPU
   d) Servers, network, backup
   Answer: b) Confidentiality, integrity, availability
8. **Which part of the risk triad ensures that data is accessible when needed?**
   a) Confidentiality
   b) Integrity
   c) Availability

d) Authenticity
Answer: c) Availability

9. **Integrity in the risk triad refers to:**
a) Encrypting all files
b) Ensuring data is not altered or tampered with
c) Allowing guest users
d) Backing up all files daily
Answer: b) Ensuring data is not altered or tampered with

---

4. Managing the Storage Infrastructure

10. **Managing storage infrastructure includes:**
a) Ignoring unused volumes
b) Monitoring performance, capacity, and security
c) Disabling alerts
d) Minimizing backups
Answer: b) Monitoring performance, capacity, and security
11. **A key objective of storage management is to:**
a) Reduce bandwidth
b) Delete old files
c) Optimize storage use and performance
d) Increase access time
Answer: c) Optimize storage use and performance

---

5. Monitoring the Storage Infrastructure

12. **What is the purpose of monitoring storage infrastructure?**
a) Increase electricity usage
b) Detect and respond to performance and security issues
c) Stop data backups
d) Track user entertainment
Answer: b) Detect and respond to performance and security issues
13. **Which of the following is a key parameter to monitor in storage infrastructure?**
a) Color depth
b) Disk latency
c) Video resolution
d) Page margin
Answer: b) Disk latency
14. **Which component should be monitored to avoid storage failure?**
a) CPU temperature
b) Power cables
c) Disk health and usage
d) Browser settings
Answer: c) Disk health and usage

---

6. Key Management Activities and Examples

15. **Which of the following is a key storage management activity?**
    a) Watching system themes
    b) Performing capacity planning
    c) Playing audio files
    d) Modifying fonts
    Answer: b) Performing capacity planning
16. **Storage tiering is an example of:**
    a) Data encryption
    b) Key management
    c) Performance optimization activity
    d) Application development
    Answer: c) Performance optimization activity
17. **Example of a capacity management activity is:**
    a) Defragmenting disk
    b) Removing cache
    c) Predicting future storage needs
    d) Formatting SSD
    Answer: c) Predicting future storage needs

---

7. Storage Management Standards and Industry Trends

18. **Which of the following is a storage management standard?**
    a) SNIA SMI-S
    b) HTML5
    c) TCP/IP
    d) PDF
    Answer: a) SNIA SMI-S
19. **SNIA stands for:**
    a) Secure Network for Internet Access
    b) Storage Networking Industry Association
    c) Smart Network Infrastructure Architecture
    d) Simple Network Interface Adapter
    Answer: b) Storage Networking Industry Association
20. **An industry trend in storage management is:**
    a) Using floppy disks
    b) Manual data sorting
    c) Adoption of Software-Defined Storage (SDS)
    d) Switching to analog systems
    Answer: c) Adoption of Software-Defined Storage (SDS)
21. **Software-Defined Storage (SDS) allows:**
    a) Only physical storage
    b) Decoupling of storage hardware from management software
    c) Backup through DVDs
    d) Direct use of operating systems for storage
    Answer: b) Decoupling of storage hardware from management software